CALL for Openness

STUDIES IN COMPUTER ASSISTED LANGUAGE LEARNING

Edited by Anna Turula

VOLUME 2

Prior to publication, the quality of the work published in this series is blind reviewed by an external referee appointed by the editor-ship. The referee is not aware of the author's name when performing the review.

Mariusz Marczak/Jarosław Krajka (eds.)

CALL for Openness

PETER LANG
EDITION

Bibliographic Information published by the Deutsche Nationalbibliothek
The Deutsche Nationalbibliothek lists this publication in the Deutsche Nationalbibliografie; detailed bibliographic data is available in the internet at http://dnb.d-nb.de.

Library of Congress Cataloging-in-Publication Data
Names: Marczak, Mariusz, editor. | Krajka, Jarosław, editor.
Title: CALL for openness / Mariusz Marczak, Jarosłalaw Krajka (eds.).
Description: Frankfurt am Main ; New York : Peter Lang, [2016] | Series: Studies in computer assisted language learning; Volume 2
Identifiers: LCCN 2016034369| ISBN 9783631672266 (Print) | ISBN 9783653067569 (E-PDF) | ISBN 9783631696439 (MOBI)
Subjects: LCSH: Language and languages--Study and teaching--Computer network resources. | Language and languages--Computer-assisted instruction. | Second language learning--Computer-assisted instruction. | Web-based instruction. | Online
Classification: LCC P53.28 .C349 2016 | DDC 418.00285--dc23 LC record available at https://lccn.loc.gov/2016034369

This publication was financially supported by the Pedagogical University of Cracow

Cover illustration: Michał Kwaterski

ISSN 2364-1339
ISBN 978-3-631-67226-6 (Print)
E-ISBN 978-3-653-06756-9 (E-PDF)
E-ISBN 978-3-631-69642-2 (EPUB)
E-ISBN 978-3-631-69643-9 (MOBI)
DOI 10.3726/978-3-653-06756-9

Peter Lang Edition is an Imprint of Peter Lang GmbH.

Peter Lang – Frankfurt am Main · Bern · Bruxelles · New York · Oxford · Warszawa · Wien

This publication has been peer reviewed.

www.peterlang.com

Table of Contents

Mariusz Marczak
Pedagogical University of Cracow, Cracow, Poland

Jarosław Krajka
Maria Curie-Skłodowska University, Lublin, Poland

Introduction

We live in an age of openness where unrestricted access to resources, including computer technology, knowledge and computerised/Web-based tools, is being valued as a prerequisite for personal development. The trend is increasingly noticeable – and desirable, at the same time – in educational settings as it contributes to making education more egalitarian, creating opportunities for final success to all, irrespective of their social and financial status. Even a quick keyword search of current educational publications confirms the shift for openness as it, *inter alia,* yields terms such as: open content, open licensing, open hardware and open courses but also open mind.

Particularly appealing in the openness of educational contexts, though, is the range of implications that open resources have for the teaching and learning process in technology-enhanced education as their merits go far beyond merely the introduction of free teaching aids. The implementation of open tools fosters the emergence of openness to new ideas: innovative methodologies, work and assessment modes and course design solutions – to name but a few – which altogether are expected to yield outcomes relevant to the lives and practices of modern-day students in the open and ever-changing world that they are being educated for.

The afore-mentioned innovations cater for a range of student needs on a number of levels, including: cognition, i.e. the internalisation of factual, declarative knowledge; behaviour, involving the development of practical skills which equip students for their future private and professional lives, and metacognitive awareness, which manifests itself in increased understanding of the learning context, the ability to reflect on, and alter, one's learning process with a view to improving the quality of its outcomes.

Interestingly enough, the incorporation of openness into the teaching/learning process additionally breeds openness to unchartered areas of research, whereby the new practices can be investigated, validated and further improved.

The purpose of this volume is to demonstrate what openness in education is and what contributions it can potentially make to teachers' and students' cognitive, behavioural and metacognitive development, basing on a number of exemplary solutions involving the use of innovative information and communication technologies, learning methods and techniques as well as work modes.

The first chapter, written by **Maria Chojnacka** and **Katarzyna Kurczak,** deals with openness towards mobility and examines how mobile technology, which functions in the cloud and is available to anyone with Internet connectivity, may be harnessed in order to augment memorisation in English for Medical Purposes university courses by increasing students' mental powers through the use of mnemonics and spaced presentation. At the same time, they indicate that mobile learning can also autonomise learners, help in sustaining their motivation levels, and simultaneously develop at least selected elements of their digital literacy. In the light of the findings presented in this chapter, it appears that the learning gains achieved through mobile-enabled instruction are multi-dimensional and may reach beyond the teacher's most immediate goals.

Agnieszka Gadomska in chapter two demonstrates how established Web-based educational tools are still open to innovative usage, and introduces a method of teaching in which Moodle, the learning management system (LMS), can be utilised in order to transform students from content users into content creators, whereby they learn how to author Computer Assisted Language Learning materials through hands-on experience. She illustrates how, in effect, students are likely to benefit from increased empowerment and changed user roles which they may be asked to play in an LMS. She focuses particularly on how the solution in question, which seems to correspond more adequately to students' expectations and needs, boosts their overall Information and Communication Technology skills, increases their motivation and expands their knowledge of methodology beyond the use of technology in foreign language instruction.

Chapter three, by **Elżbieta Gajek,** provides an example of how the utilisation of computer-aided audio-video translation (AVT) may also serve pedagogical purposes, and how techniques such as captioning and revoicing can be transformed from AVT solutions into full-fledged teaching techniques with which to ameliorate foreign language methodology. The application of AVT, which enables language learners to translate both oral and written foreign language texts, opens new educational horizons, especially with regard to course design, materials construction, teaching and learning strategies, interaction and integration patterns in the social learning situation as well as innovative assessment modes. What is more, the new teaching practices are also likely to inspire the channelling of research efforts into new areas, where the entailing learning gains may be examined and optimised.

Ferit Kiliçkaya in chapter four reviews a number of studies dealing with the concept of the use of screencasting technology for instructional purposes with a view to enhancing lecture delivery, on the one hand, and feedback provision, on the other. He tackles a number of issues which must be taken into account when using audio-augmented screen recordings in either of the modes. Finally, he presents a number of implications that the results of the studies conducted to date in the afore-mentioned area have for class preparation, materials construction and use as well as the individualisation of the teaching/learning procedures in blended and distant learning courses.

In chapter five **Przemysław Krakowian** discusses the use of Web-based open educational resources (OER) for intercultural learning. He does so by introducing CEFcult, an online learning platform designed for the purpose of fostering the development of university students' professional intercultural communication skills through self-reflection on their participation in authentic scenarios involving communication with representatives of other cultures. The platform provides Web-based communication tools, complete with validated assessment schemes for increased efficacy. As the author notes, the value of OER lies in the fact that they offer students two kinds of openness: one stems from the very nature of the resources, which is traceable in ease of access on the part of the students, while the other derives from the opportunity that online communication tools create for language classroom students to engage in genuine intercultural exchanges.

Chapter six, by **Mariusz Kruk,** investigates the extent to which opening instruction modes to those involving the use of new online tools - Web resources, including a browser-based virtual world called Yoowalk, in this case - assists teachers in lowering secondary school learners' overall anxiety and communication apprehension levels in foreign language lessons. The classroom research study discussed by the author permits him to present practical aspects of language instruction augmented by virtual worlds and provides an opportunity to speculate which factors appear likely to facilitate learning in similar settings.

Anita Buczek-Zawiła in chapter seven calls for teachers to remain open to the idea of developing students' lexical competence and pronunciation in English while attending to both meaning and form, simultaneously. She advocates the use of online dictionaries for that purpose, with the caveat that they may help teachers and students achieve their goals only on condition that they are subject to meticulous assessment prior to use. As she suggests, it is often that a combination of online dictionaries, rather than a single product, will enable instructors and students to attain success, while the very need for informed materials selection may additionally increase students' awareness of the user choices which they make pertaining to the learning aids which they decide to use.

The volume ends with chapter eight, in which **Anna Turula** discusses the results of an action research study, based on triangulated data, which delves into the delivery of hybrid tutoring, provided face-to-face and in-cloud, in the course of an MA seminar in new technologies in education. As she maintains, the merit of this kind of work mode in academic education lies in the fact that it is likely to promote an open mind in both teachers and students. In the case of the former, openness regards not only the ability to plan and administer technology-enhanced teaching procedures in an effective manner in a here-and-now situation, given the teacher's most immediate context, but also – and perhaps, first and foremost – readiness to observe and respond to constant change, reflect on the teaching and learning process as a way in which to self-develop and tailor teaching practices to particular circumstances.

We realise that the various dimensions of openness in education which this volume deals with are only a selection made out of a broader range possible. Nevertheless, we believe that they will serve as food for thought and an encouragement for teachers to strive at the most adequate kind of openness in their specific settings, regarding course design, lesson planning, the choice of materials, instructional aids and delivery models as well as assessment modes as a response to the dynamics of the present day education. We also hope that teachers will not limit themselves to considering openness as an option for themselves only, but that they will, in addition, attempt to foster an open mind and readiness for innovation in their students.

Volume editors
Mariusz Marczak
Jarosław Krajka

Maria Chojnacka
University of Social Sciences, Warsaw, Poland

Katarzyna Kurczak
Medical University of Warsaw, Warsaw, Poland

The Impact of Self-Paced Memrise-Based Homework Assignments on Enhancing Course Content Acquisition

Abstract
This research project examines the issue of technology enhancing the process of teaching English for Medical Purposes to university students. It was inspired by a strong conviction that mobile devices can be powerful educational tools. For the purpose of this study participants were asked to complete self-paced homework assignments created on Memrise, a free-of-charge online learning tool that uses flashcards augmented with mnemonics and spaced presentation. The data yielded by the study lent considerable support to the premise that the learning process was effective, and that using Memrise affected the post-test results. There was a minimum Memrise score that had to be achieved for post-test results to be improved as well as a cut-off score in Memrise, beyond which further practice was not very efficient. To facilitate a proper understanding of the results of the study, the authors focused on the areas of learner motivation and digital literacy.

Keywords: learner autonomy, spaced repetition software, mobile-assisted language learning, English for Medical Purposes, Memrise

1. Introduction

The gradually increasing access to reasonably priced portable technologies has led numerous language teachers to adopt mobile technologies into their everyday practice (Stockwell and Hubbard 2013, Oblinger and Oblinger 2005). The concept of openness, i.e. open educational resources, open access or open teaching, has had a profound influence on many areas of education (Oblinger 2012). Openness to embracing new technologies in English for Specific Purposes practice seems to be the way for educational scenarios to resemble contemporary life.

Mobile-assisted learning solutions are an emerging discipline in the area of English for Specific Purposes (ESP) education. It is important to collect research data on their use to optimise the mobile-assisted teaching of English for Medical

Purposes (EMP), a branch of ESP, as "(…) the command of English has become a key pre-requisite for doing clinical or theoretical research and taking part in international biomedical communication" (Charpy and Carnet 2014: 4).

Memrise is an educational platform where educators can create courses that are freely and openly available to learners, which allows crossing the boundaries of traditional institutional settings allowing participation by individuals not officially enrolled in the course. This paper aims to present the results of a research project exploring the process of mobile- and Memrise-enhanced learning and the teaching of English for Medical Purposes.

2. Literature review

In recent years, the concept of mobile-assisted learning has gained prominence in the field of educational research. There is a growing body of literature concerning m-learning as various forms of mobile-enhanced learning and their implementation in the educational context have been explored by researchers and educational practitioners.

2.1 Mobile-assisted (language) learning

The use of personal portable devices created an opportunity for implementing new ways of learning that are able to encompass different learning contexts and put emphasis on the continuity of the learning process (Kukulska-Hulme and Shield 2008). The notion of m-learning, as opposed to traditional study environments, has been widely discussed in the literature, e.g. Burston 2014a, 2014b; Cobcroft et al. 2006; Corbeil et al. 2007; Hall and Elliott 2003; Hoppe 2006; Ingleton et al. 2000; Jones et al. 2014; Keller 2008; Kim et al. 2006; Kukulska-Hulme 2005, 2007, 2008a, 2008b, 2008c, 2009a, 2009b, 2010a, 2010b, 2010c, 2010d, 2010e, 2012a, 2012b, 2012c, 2013a, 2013b, 2013c, 2014; 2015; Kukulska-Hulme and Traxler 2005; McCallum 2009; Newhouse 2001; Sha et al. 2012, or Traxler 2009, among others.

What distinguishes mobile-assisted language learning (MALL) from computer-assisted language learning (CALL), is the "(…) use of personal, portable devices that enable new ways of learning, emphasizing continuity or spontaneity of access and interaction across different contexts" (Kukulska-Hulme and Shield 2008: 273). Although we distinguish CALL from MALL, with an increase in the functionality of devices, greater processing speed and storage, it is becoming easier and easier to move resources across devices, and thus the boundaries between these two categories are becoming more and more blurred. With ongoing technological development, MALL has the potential to influence foreign language learning and teaching, especially once drawbacks such as small screen sizes, Internet access or data transmission speed have been overcome. Even with its obvious limitations, m-learning clearly offers a number of solutions inaccessible to conventional e-learning (Kukulska-Hulme and Traxler 2005: 181).

2.2 Research on mobile-assisted language learning

A growing interest in mobile-assisted language learning resulted not only in a plethora of MALL implementation studies but also in a considerable number of review studies related to the effectiveness of MALL solutions and the development of new pedagogies tailored to mobile learning (Park and Slater 2014), e.g. the comprehensive list of 345 MALL projects dating from 1994 to 2012 compiled by Burston (2013) should serve as a lynchpin for those interested in MALL implementations.

Mobile phones ranked first among devices used in mobile learning projects funded by the European Union (Pęcherzewska and Knot 2007, in Kukulska-Hulme and Shield 2008: 271–274). In 2008, a special issue of the ReCALL journal was devoted to mobile-assisted language learning (Shield and Kukulska-Hulme 2008). MALL solutions gained popularity and recognition in both small and large educational contexts, e.g. BBC Bitesize Mobile, MOBILearn European Project (Sharples 2006), and were widely discussed in literature, e.g. Kukulska-Hulme (2010c, 2013a, 2013c), Kukulska-Hulme and Bull (2008, 2009), Kukulska-Hulme and Shield (2008), Kukulska-Hulme, Shield and Hassan (2010), or Kukulska-Hulme and Wible (2008), among others.

While the early generation of mobile-assisted language learning offered activities that were meticulously designed by educators and engineers, nowadays, due to widespread access to mobile devices, mobile-assisted language learning is more likely to be used to support social contact and promote collaborative learning (Kukulska-Hulme and Shield 2008; Kukulska-Hulme et al. 2007; Petit and Kukulska-Hulme 2007).

With the novelty factor slowly wearing off, the last few years have brought about a critical approach towards the reality of MALL project implementation (Burston 2014a, 2014b). Review studies disclose MALL limitations, suggest future directions for MALL development and open the way to a proper understanding of the values resulting from the use of MALL solutions in education, e.g. Gajek (2015) on the use of mobile technology in language learning; Chinnery (2006) on emerging MALL technologies; Collins (2005), Kiernan and Aizawa (2004) or Kennedy and

Levy (2008) on mobile language learning with cell phones; Godwin-Jones (2011) on mobile apps for language learning; Herrington (2009) on using smartphones to create digital teaching episodes; or Herrington et al. (2009) on mobile learning in higher education, among others.

Exploratory questionnaire-based surveys into the use of mobile technologies have been conducted by many researchers, e.g. Kukulska-Hulme, Shield and Hassan (2009) or Czerska-Andrzejewska (2015), among others. State-of-the-art research provides insight into the MALL experience (Ma 2016) or student perspectives on the affordances and constraints on using mobile devices and applications for learning languages (Steel 2016). Guidelines have been offered for mobile app design for individual and sustainable MALL (Kim 2016) or for improving reading skills through instant short messages (Gutiérrez-Colón Plana et al. 2016). Cortez and Roy (2012) discuss screen interface design for MALL in the EFL context. In a similar vein, Castrillo et al. (2014), Rodríguez-Arancón et al. (2013), or Stockwell and Hubbard (2013), discuss the design and implementation of mobile and MALL apps. De Waard (2014) investigates the use of the BYOD (bring-your-own-device) method for meaningful mobile learning.

Some researchers focus on external factors affecting m-learning, e.g. Fatahipour and Ghasemninajm (2014) examine context-aware solutions in MALL, whereas others focus on learner-internal factors, e.g. learner autonomy in MALL (Diaz-Vera 2012) or the effects of student-centred m-learning on language acquisition (Oberg and Daniels 2013).

At this point, it is important to highlight that mobile-assisted language learning allows for a crossing of boundaries between the formal learning context, i.e. inside the classroom, and the informal learning context, i.e. outside the classroom (Jarvis and Achilleos 2013 after Kukulska-Hulme 2009b), and that such crossing of boundaries and out-of-class mobile support for vocabulary training lay at the foundations of our research project.

2.3 Mobile vocabulary trainers

With the growth of mobile technologies, developing technology-enhanced learning tools has become a critical issue in the field of ELT (Kukulska-Hulme and Traxler 2005; Chen and Chung 2008). There have appeared numerous online vocabulary trainers, based on item response theory, designed to support personalized vocabulary learning. Highly elaborate algorithms have been used to facilitate memorization as well as to help integrate learning into one's daily routine, challenging the notion of what had been regarded as effective in pedagogic design (e.g. Cortez and Roy 2012). Online vocabulary trainers are more and more frequently enumerated in teacher training publications (Buttner 2007; Ma et al. 2013; Presson et al. 2013). These intelligent tutor systems are steadily becoming more popular (Stockwell 2007, in Kukulska-Hulme and Shield 2008) as they allow personalized learner profiles to be created and deliver activities according to identified problem areas.

2.4 Mobile technology in teaching English for Medical Purposes

Being able to write and communicate in English has become an important career predictor for a healthcare professional (see the discussion in Basturkmen 2006; Ferguson 2013; Flowerdew 2013; Krickova and Polackova 2010; Parkinson 2000; Ribes et al. 2010; Taylor 2005, among others). There is a growing demand for doctors to be able to deliver conference presentations and papers in English as well as communicate with English-speaking patients (Iwata et al. 2014). Not surprisingly, there is exponential interest in efficient learning and teaching English for Medical Purposes (Antić 2010; Coxhead 2013; Ribes et al. 2010; Rogers 2007; Taylor 2005; Wang et al. 2008).

The healthcare branch is quite effective in developing solutions for healthcare professionals, some of which can be used in EMP practice. As EMP is a well-established branch of ESP (Hung et al. 2010), there appear many useful websites or technological solutions that non-native speakers of EMP might benefit from.

Nevertheless, there are only a few independent efficacy studies on flashcard software interventions in learning English for Medical Purposes. Schmidmaier et al. (2011) investigated the use of electronic flashcards in medical education. The study demonstrated that repetitive testing is a potent learning strategy for short-term retention, but it did not confirm the efficacy of this method for long-term knowledge retention. In a randomized, controlled study, Taveira-Gomes et al. (2015) investigated spaced-repetition and test-enhanced recall accuracy among medical students using Alert Student, a spaced-repetition flashcard platform using test-enhanced learning. Bow et al. (2013) developed a crowdsourcing learning tool for medical students to share flashcards. Exam scores analysis revealed that students who had access to the flashcard system outperformed those who did not.

The above-mentioned studies focused on medical content knowledge rather than language knowledge; therefore, it would be valuable to research the efficacy of flashcard spaced-repetition software in the context of learning English for Medical Purposes.

3. The study

3.1 Aim of the research

Guided by interest in mobile-assisted learning of foreign languages as well as a conviction that mobile phones can be considered as powerful educational devices, the authors investigated factors relevant to effective mobile-assisted learning of English for Medical Purposes. We were interested in whether a Memrise-rooted learning experience can enhance the acquisition of course content but also in the extent to which medical students are open to the use of (mobile) technology in learning English for Medical Purposes.

3.2 Participants

A total of 40 first-year medical students (25 women and 14 men) were asked to participate in the research project. Language instruction delivered to the study participants consisted of one 90-minute lesson of English for Medical Purposes per week. All students followed the same textbook and were taught by the same language teacher.

To gain insight into group dynamics the study participants were asked to fill in a pre- and a post-project questionnaire referring to learning motivation, digital literacy and attitudes to mobile-assisted language learning. The emerging picture showed a group of young people with mixed disposition towards both studying medicine and learning English for Medical Purposes. Approximately, they spend up to one hour learning English in various contexts, e.g. when commuting, and - at various times of the day - using English as a vehicle for content acquisition. They speak at least two foreign languages and are convinced that their motivation is a key factor in successful foreign language learning.

3.3 Design and procedure

The study participants were asked to sign up for Memrise (www.memrise.com), a free-of-charge online learning tool that uses flashcards augmented with mnemonics as well as spaced presentation, and complete self-paced homework assignments. The assignments were based on vocabulary sampled from the textbook followed in the classroom. In Stage 1 (Unit 3) all students were obliged to sign up for the course. Having discussed Unit 3 in the classroom, the study participants took an immediate vocabulary post-test and a delayed vocabulary post-test which was designed in such a way so as to constitute a part of the end-of-term test covering Units 1 to 3.

The assumption was that having completed an obligatory Memrise-based course, the participants would be familiar with the program, so that Memrise would not pose difficulty as a learning tool itself in Stage 2 of the research project. Such design of the research project would additionally help to eliminate the novelty factor in Memrise usage. Stage 2 (Unit 5) also involved self-paced Memrise-based homework assignments; however, the course mode was changed to voluntary self-paced homework. Students could enrol in the course after completing a vocabulary pre-test. Subsequently, Unit 5 content was discussed in the classroom and then followed by a vocabulary post-test.

Data for the study were collected in the academic year 2014–2015. Statistical analysis was performed by means of the IBM SPSS version 20 for Windows.

3.4 Results and discussion

3.4.1 Acquisition of course content

We examined what progress students made in learning the course content by comparing the results of the Unit 5 pre-test with the results of the post-test administered after Unit 5. For that purpose a paired sample one-tailed directional t-test was used. The t value (-2.41) showed that the mean in the post-test (22.9) was significantly higher than the mean in the pre-test (10.45). The results are shown in Table 1.

Table 1. Mean equality test

	Mean	N	t	p (one-tailed)
U5 pre-test	10.45	40	-2.41	0.01
U5 post-test	22.90	40		

The results supported the conclusion that the learning process was effective. The next issue to investigate was whether the use of Memrise affected test results. To address this issue, correlations between scores in Memrise and post-tests were examined in two different scenarios: 1) when Memrise usage was obligatory (Unit 3) and 2) when Memrise usage was voluntary (Unit 5). In both cases high scores in Memrise correlated with high test results. However, what is interesting, as far as voluntary Memrise usage is concerned, the correlation was decidedly higher and significant at a higher level (tau=0.5, p <0.001, df=36, whereas in obligatory usage tau=0.34, p<0.01, df=38).

As correlation results make the relation between Memrise usage (based on the number of Memrise points collected by the study participants, i.e. Memrise score) and test results very probable, it seemed interesting to check whether there was a minimal level of Memrise score which should be gained to improve the overall test score (the analysis was performed for Unit 3).

The analysis showed the level of 50,000 Memrise points as a minimum Memrise score that needed to be achieved for Memrise usage to influence test results, as shown in Table 2.

Table 2. Results in U3 post-test for groups with/without minimum in Memrise U3

Group	N	U3 post-test Mean	t	p (one-tailed)
Below 50,000 in Memrise U3	7	26.07	-2.934	0.003
Above 50,000 in Memrise U3	33	40.85		

A similar analysis was performed in search of a maximum Memrise score, where further learning did not improve the post-test results. The analysis showed that the level of 85,000 points could be considered as a cut-off point beyond which more Memrise activity did not lead to better test results. The results are shown in Table 3.

Table 3. Results in U3 post-test for groups with/without maximum in Memrise U3

Group	N	U3 post-test Mean	t	p (one-tailed)
Below 85,000 in Memrise U3	27	36.15	-1.48	0.07
More than 85,000 in Memrise U3	13	42.65		

A regression analysis was performed to determine whether self-paced Memrise-based homework assignments enhanced the acquisition of course material. The results showed that both scores, i.e. in Memrise for Unit 5 and for Unit 3, were important in predicting the Unit 5 post-test scores. Interestingly, the end-of-term test results turned out to be one of the predictors, while Unit 5 pre-test results were not (see Table 4).

Table 4. Regression analysis of the post-test results in Unit 5

	standardized beta	t	p (2-tailed)	partial correlations
Constant	-	.437	0.665	
Memrise U3 score	-0.392	-4.25	0.000	-0.62
U3 task in the end-of-term test	0.195	2.25	0.03	0.39
U5 pre-test	0.131	1.47	0.15	0.26
Memrise U5 score	0.870	9.592	0.000	0.87

Perhaps a central conclusion to be drawn is that Memrise usage was the most important factor determining the students' success, or the lack of it. It could also be hypothesized that the voluntary usage of Memrise was an expression of a general motivation for learning English, which, on the other hand, could be seen in the involvement in course activity in Unit 3 and the end-of-term test results.

An additional analysis of correlation showed that Memrise scores in Unit 3 and Unit 5 correlated positively, but not on a significant level (tau=0.17), while Unit 3 task results in the end-of-term test correlated both with Memrise Unit 3 and Unit 5 scores (0.56, $p<0.001$ and tau=0.27, $p<0.05$, respectively). The correlations and beta scores support – at least to a degree – the above-mentioned hypothesis about the impact of students' general motivation on various aspects of learning and its results. It could also be said that Memrise Unit 5 score is an effect of general motivation and active here-and-now variables which were not observed in the study, e.g. difficulty of other exams, personal situation, etc.

Figure 1. The prediction of the post-test results

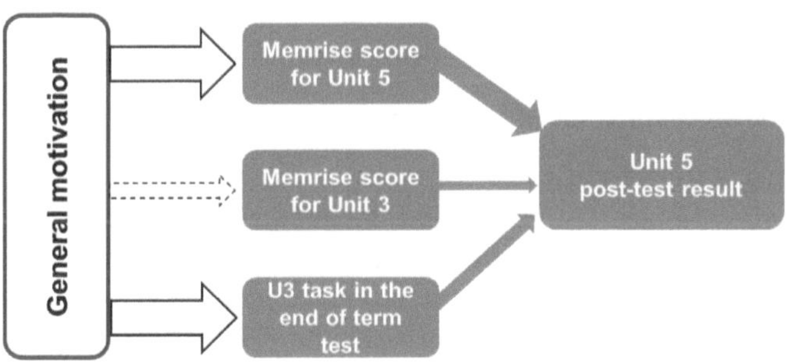

In other words, although the results point to Memrise usage as a crucial factor determining success in the Unit 5 post-test, we might assume that it was an expression of general attitude towards learning, which could be observed also in the end-of-term test results. However, as the result of the end-of-term test was not significant as a predictor of the Unit 5 post-test results, it could be said that motivation is not enough, and to achieve a good result students need to make at least a minimal level of effort (see Table 2 with minimum Memrise score).

Consequently, we might assume that those students who had a relatively high Memrise score in Unit 5 and good results in U3 task in the end-of-term test would obtain the highest post-test scores in Unit 5. It could also be assumed that there should emerge a hierarchy of results, i.e. Group 1 would achieve the best results, and Group 4 would achieve the worst results. To check this reasoning, the sample was divided depending on scores in Memrise (High/Low) and performance in the end-of-term test (High/Low).

The results confirmed the reasoning presented above: there was a hierarchy of the U5 post-test results (see Table 5). Moreover, t-tests showed that differences between Groups 1 and 2 were statistically significant ($t=4.79$, $p<0.001$). Thus, only general motivation to learn supported by actual effort seems to lead to the best learning results.

Table 5. U5 post-test performance in sub-groups chosen on the basis of U5 Memrise score and U3 task in the end-of-term test results

Group No	N	U5 Memrise	U3 task in the end of term test	U5 post-test Mean	U5 Post-test SD
1	10	High	High	41.8	18.18
2	9	High	Low	11.8	4.74
3	14	Low	High	10.7	5.91
4	5	Low	Low	9.0	10.15

At this point it can be quite convincingly argued that:

1) The learning process was effective.
2) Memrise usage affected post-test results, and the impact of voluntary usage was probably higher than that of obligatory usage (which was probably related to motivational interference).
3) There was a minimum Memrise score that had to be achieved for post-test results to be improved.
4) There was a cut-off score in Memrise, beyond which further practice was not very efficient.

Figure 2. Probable relation between voluntarily used Memrise and test scores (regression curve estimation)

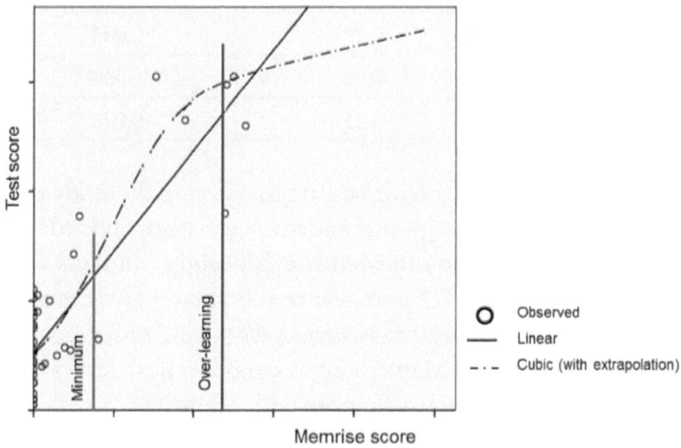

3.4.2 *Memrise usage*

As signalled before, Memrise usage for Unit 5 was voluntary. It was then of fundamental interest to discover what led some of the study participants to use or abandon Memrise as an educational tool. An additional variable, called 'test', was calculated as a mean result in three tests: in U3 immediate post-test task, U3 task in the end-of-term test and the end-of-term test. The analysis showed that both Memrise U3 score and new variables were significant predictors of the scores in voluntary Unit 5 Memrise usage (see Table 6).

Table 6. Regression analysis of Memrise voluntary use

	Standardized beta	**t**	**p**
(Constant)		-2.88	0.01
U3 Memrise score	0.359	2.45	0.02
test	0.321	2.19	0.04

It might have been the case that Memrise itself was not captivating enough for students to use it. The analysis of correlations showed that self-motivation was the main factor influencing Memrise usage, and the application was captivating to a moderate extent.

Table 7. Correlation between 'test' variable and Memrise scores

	tau	p (one-tailed)
U3 Memrise score	0.29	0.004
U5 Memrise score	0.28	0.009
Sum of Memrise scores	0.41	0.000

While investigating the issue of whether Memrise attractiveness to the study participants would be of relevance to pedagogy, the students were again divided into four groups. If the study participants found Memrise appealing, students who had high U3 Memrise scores and high U3 post-test results should also have the highest U5 Memrise scores. If the assumption is wrong, we should observe some changes, as those students who had low Memrise scores and low post-test results could change their attitude and decide to work more with Memrise.

The results (see Table 8) demonstrate that there was a clear hierarchy of U5 Memrise scores. There was no significant modification of student behaviour, and those who were good in Memrise Unit 3 remained good in Memrise Unit 5; on the other hand, those who were poor in Memrise Unit 3, stayed poor in Memrise Unit 5.

Table 8. Scores in U5 Memrise in sub-groups chosen on the basis of Memrise U3 score and U3 post-test performance

Group	N	U3 Memrise	U3 post-test	U5 Memrise Mean	U5 Memrise SD
1	10	High	High	75.495	75.273
2	11	High	Low	20.355	40.123
3	10	Low	High	6.743	13.327
4	9	Low	Low	2.733	5.498

The average score in Unit 3 immediate post-test (0.63) was visibly higher than the one in Unit 5 immediate post-test (0.26). As Memrise use was not the only difference (e.g. a slight difference in Unit content difficulty was a disturbance variable), we could not attribute the whole difference pointed by the t-test result to Memrise only. Nevertheless, as the achievement of a minimum score in Memrise was one of the factors in test success, it makes it very plausible that Memrise performance, or, in other words, work/time invested in learning via the application, influenced post-test results in both cases.

To conclude, the data discussed indicate that the usage of Memrise was related to some general factor – which could be composed of attitude towards learning English, motivation, abilities, attitudes towards mobile-assisted language learning. etc. What is more, a number of Memrise U5 Non-Users voiced an opinion that Memrise helped them organize their learning better; however, it might be the case that those students who despite impending medical exams found time to do the Memrise course were better organised anyway, and Memrise usage did not have such a significant impact on their learning habits.

3.4.3 *Attitudes towards MALL*

At baseline, 84 % of students agreed or strongly agreed that mobile devices are easy to use (see Figure 3) and 64 % of the study participants declared that a mobile phone is a convenient device to learn English for Medical Purposes (see Figure 4). However, the majority of the study participants reported modest or no experience with mobile-assisted language learning.

Figure 3. Mobile devices are easy to use

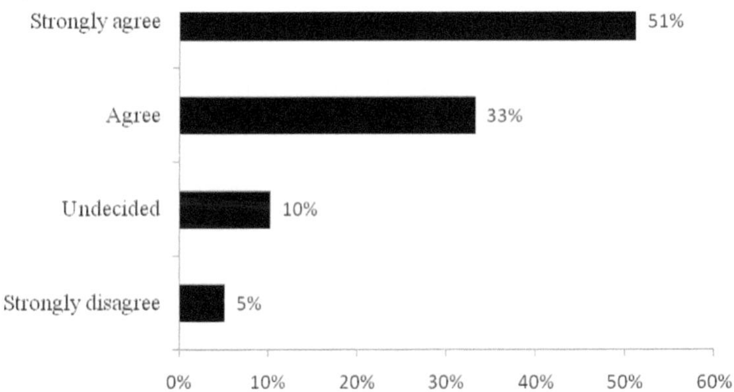

Nearly one-third (28 %) of the study participants were undecided whether a mobile phone is a convenient device to learn English for Medical Purposes. Two students (5 %) strongly disagreed with the statement, which might suggest that there was a small group of students who did not enjoy using mobile devices in general, and that objection extended to learning via mobile devices as well.

Figure 4. A mobile phone is a convenient tool to learn English for Medical Purposes

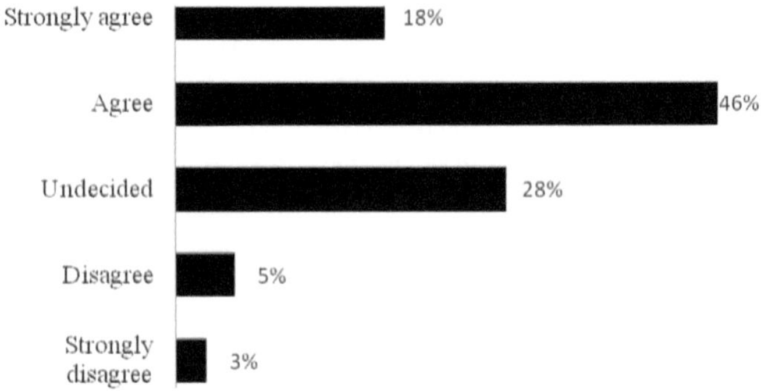

It is worth reminding at this point that three students reported that their mobile phones did not support the use of mobile applications, thus some of the students might have disagreed with the claim on technical and not ideological grounds. What is more, the majority of the study participants reported limited free of charge data transfer in their mobile devices resulting in the willingness to access free Wi-Fi whenever possible, which might have influenced their judgement of mobile-assisted language learning.

After the educational experience with Memrise the study participants were asked to rank it on a scale from 1 to 5, where 1 was the lowest score and 5 was the highest score. As can be seen in Figure 5, the overall grade in the U5 Users group was 4.5. In the Memrise U5 Non-Users group, the overall grade was 4.2. The overall grade for Memrise, according to users who downloaded the mobile application from Google Play Store (1 million downloads; ranked by 45,706 users; date of access: 18th July 2015) is 4.6. None of the study participants, even among Memrise U5 Non-Users, awarded less than 3 points. Therefore, it seems that even Memrise U5 Non-Users were moderately satisfied with Memrise and the reason for not using Memrise for Unit 5 did not lie only in Memrise itself. This claim is partially supported by the reasons the Memrise U5 Non-Users provided for not attending the Memrise U5 course, i.e. lack of time (8 responses), no Internet access (1 response), having forgotten to do so (1 response), other duties/other university classes to pass (3 responses) and low motivation (1 response).

Figure 5. Memrise overall grade

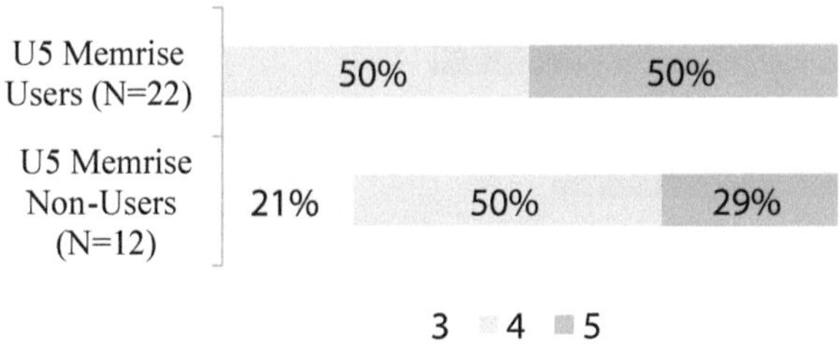

As far as attitudes towards mobile-assisted language learning are concerned, more Memrise U5 Users reported that the mobile version of Memrise was easier to use than the regular desktop/laptop version (3.6 vs. 3.3 on a 1-to-5 Likert scale, respectively). When the participants were asked whether they consider a smartphone a convenient tool, the grade was 4.0 for Memrise U5 Users and 4.3 for Memrise U5 Non-Users.

At the preliminary stage of the research project, 51 % of the study participants stated that they preferred mobile devices to a desktop computer, 18 % of the study participants stated the contrary, and nearly 31 % of the study participants did not have a clear view on the matter. Also, 64 % of the study participants thought that a smartphone is a convenient tool for learning English for Medical Purposes. That number increased to 77 % in the post-project questionnaire, and the number of the undecided decreased by nearly 8 %. One student (3 %) strongly disagreed with the statement both before and after the project; nevertheless, the number of participants who disagreed with the statement dropped to zero. The overall grade for that question before the research project was 3.71, whereas after the research project it was 4.0 for Memrise U5 Users and 4.3 for Memrise U5 Non-Users.

Figure 6. A smartphone is a convenient tool for learning English for Medical Purposes

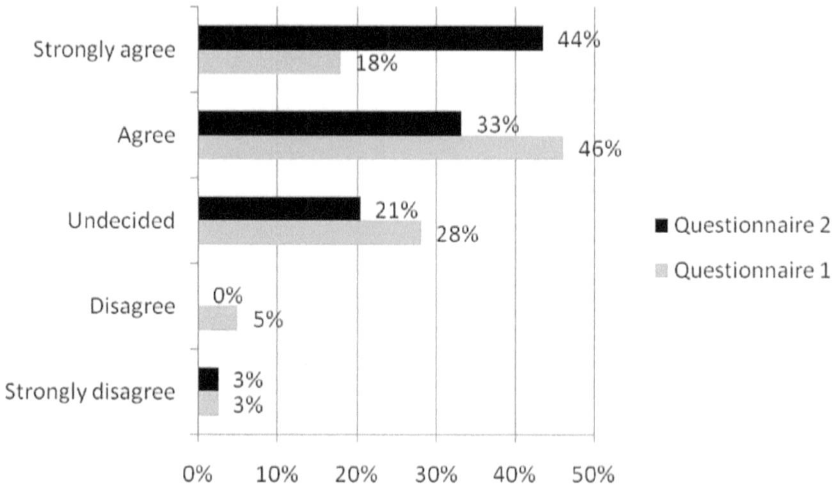

The overall grade for mobile-assisted language learning convenience and efficiency improved from 3.6 to 4.0 and 4.5 for Memrise Unit 5 Users and Memrise Unit 5 Non-Users, respectively. Therefore, the use of a smartphone itself as an educational tool was not the reason for opting out of the Memrise course.

Data from student responses before and after the research project demonstrate that the number of the study participants who after the educational experience with Memrise considered a smartphone to be a convenient tool for learning English for Medical Purposes increased by 13 %. Memrise U5 Users were less generous when grading Memrise features, probably due to the fact that they had spent more time learning via Memrise and were more exposed to its shortcomings. The mobile device itself as an educational tool appeared not to be the reason for opting out of the course. The Memrise opt-out factor might have been influenced by the co-occurrence of crucial medical exams, drawing student attention away from learning English for Medical Purposes towards studying medical content subjects. Although a number of students voiced an opinion that Memrise helped them organize their learning better and they would recommend it to other medical students, test and Memrise performance related data demonstrated that only having a general motivation to learn supported by actual effort (a sufficient Memrise score) leads to the best learning results, as measured by the post-test.

3.5 Limitations of the study

The current study has limitations that should be acknowledged. As the study focused on a specific instructional context, i.e. first-year medical students learning English for Medical Purposes, the findings are not generalizable to other contexts. Moreover, a small number of participants and short duration of experimental method are a major limitation. Nevertheless, despite missing data resulting from lack of some of the test scores and in one case inability to assign the Memrise score to a particular study participant, hopefully due diligence was exercised in keeping with academic and analytical standards.

3.6 Directions for the future

Mobile learning solutions should emerge in the process of interaction between software developers, teachers and end users (see the discussion on the quality criteria for educational applications in Rodriguez-Aracón et al. 2013). Following Turula (2015), the authors strongly believe that it is research-informed pedagogy that should be the driving force for innovative technology-enhanced educational practices, and not technology itself.

Therefore, informed by the data obtained, we find it important to emphasize that although mobile-assisted language learning via Memrise has the potential to, at worst, decrease test preparation time, and at best, transform English for Medical Purposes practice, the situation calls for educational solutions tailored to the needs of medical students. Adjusting the existing applications to the needs of medical students may not be sufficient, and perhaps a new learning application should be designed to respond to these unique needs and at the same time find the "(…) balance between the timeless and the up-to-date" (Turula 2015: 91).

References

Allegra, Mario – Giovanni Fulantelli – Manuel Gentile – Davide Taibi (eds.)
2008 *Emerging Educational Technologies and Practices.* Palermo: Consiglio Nazionale delle Ricerche, Instituto per le Tecnologie Didattiche.

Antić, Zorica
2010 "Analysis of Student's Errors in English for Medical Purposes", *Scientific Journal of the Faculty of Medicine in Niš, 27*(3), 159–163.

Basturkmen, Helen
2006 *Ideas and Options in English for Specific Purposes.* Mahwah, New Jersey, London: Lawrence Erlbaum Associates Publishers.

Berge, Zane L. – Lin Y. Muilenburg (eds.)
2013 *Handbook of Mobile Learning*. New York: Routledge.

Bow, Hansen C. – Jonathan R. Dattilo – Andrea M. Jonas – Christoph U. Lehmann
2013 "A crowdsourcing model for creating preclinical medical education study tools", *Acad Med. 88*(6), 766–770. Available at: doi: 10.1097/ACM.0b013e31828f86ef (date of access: 13 November 2015).

Burston, Jack
2013 "Mobile-assisted language learning: A selected annotated bibliography of implementation studies 1994–2012", *Language Learning and Technology, 17*(3), 157–225.
2014a "A survey of MALL curriculum integration: What the published research doesn't tell", *CALICO Journal, 31*(3), 303–322. Available at: doi:10.11139/cj.31.3.303-322 (date of access: 13 November 2015).
2014b "The reality of MALL project implementations: Still on the fringes", *CALICO Journal 31*(1), 43–65. Available at: doi:10.11139/cj.31.1.103-125 (date of access: 13 November 2015).

Buttner Zimmer, Amy
2007 *Activities, Games and Assessment Strategies for the World Languages Classroom*. New York, London: Routledge.

Castrillo Maria-Dolores – Elena Bárcena – Antonio Pareja-Lora
2014 "Preliminary conclusions after the design and implementation of mobile learning apps for professionals", in Sake Jager – Linda Bradley – Estelle Meima – Sylvie Thouësny (eds.), 40–46.

Chapelle, Carol A.
2013 *The Encyclopedia of Applied Linguistics*. New York: Wiley.

Charpy, Jean-Pierre – Didier Carnet
2014 "The European sTANDEM Project for Certification in Medical English: Standards, acceptability and transgression(s)", *ILCEA 19/2014*. Available at: http://ilcea.revues.org/2475 (date of access 12th October 2014).

Chen, Chih-Ming – Ching-Ju Chung
2008 "Personalized mobile English vocabulary learning system based on item response theory and learning memory cycle", *Computers & Education, 51*, 624–645.

Chinnery, George M.
2006 "Emerging technologies. Going to the MALL: mobile assisted language learning", *Language Learning & Technology, 10*(1), 9–16.

Cobcroft, Rachel S. - Stephen Towers – Judith Smith – Axel Bruns
2006 "Mobile learning in review: Opportunities and challenges for learners, teachers, and institutions". *Proceedings of the Online Learning and Teaching Conference (OLT)*, Brisbane: Queensland University of Technology.

Available at: http://core.ac.uk/download/pdf/10876464.pdf (date of access: 25 October 2015).

Collins, Timothy G.
2005 "English class on the air: Mobile language learning with cell phones". *The fifth IEEE international conference on advanced learning technologies (ICALT'05)*, 402–403.

Corbeil, Rene – Cheng-Chang Pan – Michael Sullivan – Janice Butler
2007 "Enhancing e-learning through m-learning: Are you ready to go mobile?", in C. Crawford (ed.), 273–280.

Cortez, Ruth Patricia – Debopriyo Roy
2012 "Screen interface design for mobile-assisted language learning in EFL context: A case study in Japan", *Journal of Language Teaching and Research, 3*(3), 353–368.

Coxhead, Averil
2013 "Vocabulary in ESP", in Brian Paltridge – Sue Starfield (eds.), 115–132.

Crawford C. (ed.)
2007 *Proceedings of Society for Information Technology & Teacher Education (SITE)* International Conference, Chesapeake, VA: AACE, 273–280.

Czerska-Andrzejewska
2015 "Urządzenia mobilne w nauczaniu języka angielskiego jako języka obcego – badanie przeprowadzone wśród studentów", in Elżbieta Gajek (ed.), 64–82.

de Waard, Inge
2014 "Using BYOD, mobile social media, apps, and sensors for meaningful mobile learning", in Mohamed Ally – Avgoustos Tsinakos (eds.). Available at: http://www.col.org/PublicationDocuments/pub_Mobile%20 Learning_web.pdf (date of access: 20 November 2015).

Díaz-Vera, Javier E.
2012 *Left to My Own Devices: Learner Autonomy and Mobile-Assisted Language Learning. Language and Linguistics Special E-Book Collection, 2007–2012, 6.* Bingley: Emerald Group Publishing Limited.

Fatahipour, Majid – Mahnaz Ghasemninajm
2014 "A context-aware solution in mobile language learning", in Jager, Sake – Linda Bradley – Estelle J. Meima – Sylvie Thouësny (eds.), 83–87.

Ferguson, Gibson
2013 "English for Medical Purposes", in Brian Paltridge – Sue Starfield (eds.), 243–265.

Flowerdew, Lynne
2013 "Needs analysis and curriculum development in ESP", in Brian Paltridge and Sue Starfield (eds.), 325–346.

Gajek, Elżbieta (ed.)
2015 *Technologie mobilne w kształceniu językowym*. Warszawa: Texter.

Gimeno-Sanz, Ana (ed.)
2010 *New Trends in Computer-Assisted Language Learning: Working Together*. Gandia: Macmillan ELT.

Gimeno-Sanz, Ana – Mike Levy Françoise Blin – David Barr (eds.)
2016 *WorldCALL – Sustainability and Computer Assisted Language Learning*. London, New York: Bloomsbury.

Godwin-Jones, Robert
2011 "Mobile apps for language learning", *Language Learning & Technology, 15*(2), 2–11. Available at: http://llt.msu.edu/issues/june2011/emerging.pdf (date of access: 15 November 2015).

Gutiérrez-Colón Plana, Mar – Ana Gimeno – Christine Appel – Joseph Hopkins
2016 "Improving learners' reading skills through instant short messages: A sample study using WhatsApp", in Ana Gimeno-Sanz – Mike Levy – Françoise Blin – David Barr (eds.), 266–284.

Hall, Mark – Kevin N. Elliott
2003 "Diffusion of technology into the teaching process: Strategies to encourage faculty members to embrace the laptop environment", *Journal of Education for Business, 78*(6), 301–307.

Herrington, Anthony
2009 "Using a smartphone to create digital teaching episodes as resources in adult education", in Ian Herrington – Anthony Herrington – Jessica Mantei – Ian Olney – Brian Ferry (eds.), 28–35.

Herrington, Ian – Anthony Herrington – Jessica Mantei – Ian Olney – Brian Ferry (eds.)
2009 *New Technologies, New Pedagogies: Mobile Learning in Higher Education*. University of Woollongong: Faculty of Education.

Hoppe, Ulrich
2006 "How can we integrate mobile devices with broader educational scenarios?", in Mike Sharples 2006 (ed.), 31–34.

Hung, Hsuan – Jing-Jane Tsai – Pi-Ching Chen
2010 "Temporal conjunctions in medical case presentations: Examples from case presentations by native and Taiwanese physicians", *The International Journal of Interdisciplinary Social Sciences, 5*(2), 255–263.

Ingleton, Christine – Margaret Kiley – Robert Cannon Tim Rogers
2000 "Leap into… Student-centred learning". Adelaide: The University of Adelaide. Available at: https://www.imt.liu.se/en/edu/Bologna/SCL/StudentCentredLearning.pdf (date of access: 15 November 2015).

Iwata, Jun – Yuko Tamaki – Wang Shudong – John Telloyan Yuri Ajiki – John Clayton
2014 "Medical students' perceptions of using mobile phones for their English study", in Sake Jager – Linda Bradley – Estelle J. Meima – Sylvie Thouësny (eds.), 172–178.

Jager, Sake – Linda Bradley – Estelle J. Meima – Sylvie Thouësny (eds.)
2014 *CALL Design: Principles and Practice. Proceedings of the 2014 EUROCALL Conference, Gronigen, The Netherlands*. Available at: http://research-publishing.net/display_article.php?doi=10.14705/rpnet.2014.000213 (date of access: 26th June 2015).

Jarvis, Huw – Marianna Achilleos
2013 "From Computer Assisted Language Learning (CALL) to Mobile Assisted Language Use (MALU)", *The Electronic Journal for English as a Second Language, 16*(4). Available at: http://www.teslej.org/wordpress/issues/volume16/ej64/ej64a2/ (date of access: 8th August 2015).

Jones, Ann – Mark Gaved – Agnes Kukulska-Hulme – Eileen Scanlon – Charlie Pearson – Petros Lameras – Ian Dunwell – Jan Jones
2014 "Creating coherent incidental learning journeys on smartphones using feedback and progress indicators", *International Journal of Mobile and Blended Learning, 6*(4), 75–92.

Keller, John
2008 "First principles of motivation to learn and e-learning", *Distance Education, 29*(2), 175–185.

Kennedy, Claire – Mike Levy
2008 "L'italiano al telefonino: Using SMS to support beginners' language learning", *ReCALL Journal, 20*(3), 315–330. Available at: doi:10.1017/S0958344008000530 (date of access: 15 November 2015).

Kiernan, Patrick J. – Kazumi Aizawa
2004 "Cell phones in task based learning: Are cell phones useful language learning tools?", *ReCALL Journal,* 16(1), 71–84.

Kim, Heyoung
2016 "Mobile app design for individual and sustainable MALL: Implications from an empirical analysis", in Ana Gimeno-Sanz – Mike Levy – Françoise Blin – David Barr (eds.), 244–265.

Kim, Sang Hyun – Clif Mims – Kerry K. Holmes
2006 "An introduction to current trends and benefits of mobile wireless technology use in higher education", *AACE Journal, 14*(1), 77–100.

Krickova, Zuzana – Gabriela Polackova
2010 "Meeting ESP needs of nursing students at university level: Theory and practice of ESP language teaching in nursing students at Jessenius Faculty of Medicine in Martin Slovakia", *The International Journal of Interdisciplinary Social Sciences*, 5(5), 219–226.

Kukulska-Hulme, Agnes
2005 "Reading course materials in e-book form and on mobile devices", in Agnes Kukulska-Hulme – John Traxler (eds.), 125–132.
2007 "Mobile usability in educational contexts: What have we learnt?", *International Review of Research in Open and Distance Learning* 8(2), 1–16.
2008a "Human factors and innovation with mobile devices", in T. Hansson (ed.), 392–403.
2008b "Encyclopedic knowledge in the mobile age", in Gill Needham – Ally Mohamed (eds.), 29–36.
2008c "What should we do with Jack-in-the-box? Anticipating surprises in mobile learning", in Allegra, Mario – Giovanni Fulantelli – Manuel Gentile – Davide Taibi (eds.), 7–18.
2009a "Conclusions: Future directions in researching mobile learning", in Giasemi Vavoula – Norbert Pachler – Agnes Kukulska-Hulme (eds.), 353–365.
2009b "Will mobile learning change language learning?", *ReCALL,* 21(2), 157–165.
2010a *Mobile Learning for Quality Education and Social Inclusion.* UNESCO Institute for Information Technologies in Education, Moscow, Russian Federation. Available at: http://oro.open.ac.uk/31256/ (date of access: 10 December 2015).
2010b "Mobile learning as a catalyst for change", *Open Learning: The Journal of Open and Distance Learning, 25*(3), 181–185.
2010c "Charting unknown territory: Models of participation in mobile language learning", *International Journal of Mobile Learning and Organisation, 4*(2), 116–129.
2010d "Mobile learning: Using portable technologies to create new learning", *Special Issue of Open Learning, 25*(3), 181–185.
2010e "Learning cultures on the move: Where are we heading?", *Journal of Educational Technology and Society, 13*(4), 4–14.
2012a "Language learning defined by time and place: A framework for next generation designs", in Javier Díaz-Vera (ed.), 1–13.

2012b "Smart devices or people? A mobile learning quandary", *International Journal of Learning and Media, 4*(3–4), 73–77.

2012c "How should the higher education workforce adapt to advancements in technology for teaching and learning?", *The Internet and Higher Education,* 15(4), 247–254.

2013a "Re-skilling language learners for a mobile world." Monterey, CA: The International Research Foundation for English Language Education. Available at: http://www.tirfonline.org/english-in-the-workforce/mobile-assisted-language-learning/ (date of access: 15 November 2015).

2013b "Mobile learners: Who are they and who will they become?", in Zane, L. Berge – Lin, Y. Muilenburg (eds.), 145–154.

2013c "Mobile-assisted language learning", in Carol Chapelle (ed.), 3701–3709.

2014 "Mobile, wearable, companionable: Emerging technological challenges and incentives for learning", Jogos e Mobile Learning 2014, Coimbra, Portugal, Centro de Investigação em Educação (CIEd), 12–15.

2015 "Language as a bridge connecting formal and informal language learning through mobile devices", in Lung-Hsiang Wong – Marcelo Milrad – Marcus Specht (eds.), 281–294.

Kukulska-Hulme, Agnes – Susan Bull

2008 "Theoretical perspectives on mobile language learning diaries and noticing for learners, teachers and researchers", *Proceedings of the mLearn 2008 Conference, Ironbridge Gorge, Shropshire, UK.* Available at: http://oro.open.ac.uk/15105/2/384A7259.pdf (date of access: 15 November 2015).

2009 "Theory-based support for mobile language learning: Noticing and recording", *International Journal of Interactive Mobile Technologies, 3*(2), 12–18.

Kukulska-Hulme, Agnes – Lesley Shield

2008 "An overview of mobile assisted language learning: From content delivery to supported collaboration and interaction", *ReCALL, 20*(3), 271–289.

Kukulska-Hulme Agnes – Lesley Shield – Xaviere Hassan

2009 "MALL Survey Summary of Results 1 July 2009" Available at: http://kn.open.ac.uk/public/document.cfm?docid=12514 (date of access: 15 December 2015).

2010 "Mobile technologies for language learning and teaching: An exploratory investigation", in Ana Gimeno-Sanz (ed.), 167–174.

Kukulska-Hulme, Agnes – John Traxler – John Petit

2007 "Designed and user-generated activity in the mobile age", *Journal of Learning Design, 2*(1), 52–65.

Kukulska-Hulme, Agnes – John Traxler (eds.)

2005 *Mobile Learning: A Handbook for Educators and Trainers.* London and New York: Routledge.

Kukulska-Hulme, Agnes – David Wible
2008 "Context at the crossroads of language learning and mobile learning", *ICCE 2008 Workshop Proceedings, Taiwan*. Available at: http://oro.open.ac.uk/13053/1/workshop_paper1.pdf (date of access: 20 October 2015).

Ma, Quing
2016 "An evidence-based study of Hong-Kong university students' mobile-assisted language learning (MALL) experience", in Ana Gimeno-Sanz – Mike Levy – Françoise Blin – David Barr (eds.), 211–229.

Ma, Minhua – Manuel Frandinho Oliveira – Sobah Petersen – Jannicke Baalsrud Hauge (eds.)
2013 *Serious games development and applications. Proceedings of 4th International Conference, SGDA 2013*, Trondheim: Springer.

MacCallum, Kathryn
2009 "Student characteristics and variables that determine mobile learning adoption: An initial study". *Proceedings of the Universal College of Learning: Teaching and Learning Conference, Palmerston North, NZ*. Available at: http://akoaotearoa.ac.nz/download/ng/file/group-3740/n3750-student-characteristics-and-variablesthat-determine-mobile-learning-adoption---an-initial-study---mac-callum.pdf (date of access: 15 July 2015).

Needham, Gill – Ally Mohamed (eds.)
2008 *M-libraries: Libraries on the Move to Provide Virtual Access*. London: Facet Publishing.

Newhouse, Paul C.
2001 "A follow-up study of students using portable computers at a secondary school", *British Journal of Educational Technology 32*(2), 209–219. Available at: doi: 10.1111/1467-8535.00191 (date of access: 14 August 2015).

Oberg, Andrew – Paul Daniels
2013 "Analysis of the effect a student-centred mobile learning instructional method has on language acquisition", *Computer Assisted Language Learning, 26*(2), 177–196.

Oblinger, Diana G. (ed.)
2012 *Game Changers. Education and Information Technologies*. Boulder: EDUCAUSE.

Oblinger, Diana G. – James L. Oblinger (eds.)
2005 Educating the Net Generation. Boulder: EDUCAUSE. Available at: https://net.educause.edu/ir/library/pdf/pub7101.pdf (date of access: 5 September 2015).

Paltridge, Brian – Sue Starfield (eds.)
2013 *The Handbook of English for Specific Purposes*. Chichester: Wiley-Blackwell.

Park, Moonyoung – Tammy Slater
2014 "A typology of tasks for mobile-assisted language learning: Recommendation from a small-scale needs analysis", *TESL Canada Journal 13*, Special Issue 8.

Parkinson, Jean
2000 "Acquiring scientific literacy through content and genre: A theme-based language course for science students", *English for Specific Purposes, 19*, 369–387.

Petit John – Agnes Kukulska-Hulme
2007 "Going with the grain: Mobile devices in practice", *Australasian Journal of Educational Technology, 23*(1), 17–33.

Pęcherzewska, A – S. Knot
2007 *Review of Existing EU Projects Dedicated to Dyslexia, Gaming in Education and M learning*. WR08 Report to CallDysc project.

Presson, Nora – Colleen Davy – Brian MacWhitnney
2013 "Experimentalized CALL for adult second language learners", in John Schwieter (ed.), 139–164.

Ribes, Ramon – Pedro J. Aranda – John Giba
2010 *Surgical English*. Heidelberg, Dordrecht, London, New York: Springer.

Rodriguez-Arancón, Pilar – Jorge Arús – Cristina Calle
2013 "The use of current mobile learning applications in EFL", *Procedia – Social and Behavioural Sciences, 103*, 1189–1196.

Rogers, Silvia M.
2007 *Mastering Scientific and Medical Writing. A Self-help Guide*. Berlin, Heidelberg, New York: Springer.

Schmidmaier, Ralph – Rene Ebersbach – Miriam Schiller – Inga Hege – Matthias Holzer – Martin R. Fischer
2011 "Using electronic flashcards to promote learning in medical students: Retesting versus restudying", *Medical Education, 45*(11), 1101–1110.

Sha, Li – Chee-Kit Looi – Weisha Chen – Baohui Zhang
2012 "Understanding mobile learning from the perspective of self-regulated learning", *Journal of Computer Assisted Learning* 28(4), 366–378. Available at: doi: 10.1111/j.1365-2729.2011.00461.x (date of access: 15 July 2015).

Sharples, Mike (ed.)
2006 *Big Issues in Mobile Learning. Report of a Workshop by the Kaleidoscope Network of Excellence Mobile Learning Initiative*, UK: University of Nottingham.

Shield, Lesley – Agnes Kukulska-Hulme
2008 *Special Issue of ReCALL on Mobile-Assisted Language Learning*. Cambridge: Cambridge University Press.

Steel, Caroline
2016 "Students' perspectives on the affordances and constraints of using mobile devices and applications for learning languages", in Ana Gimeno-Sanz – Mike Levy – Françoise Blin – David Barr (eds.), 230–243.

Stockwell, Glen
2007 "Vocabulary on the move: investigating an intelligent mobile phone-based vocabulary tutor". *Computer Assisted Language Learning, 20*(4), 365–383.

Stockwell, Glen – Philip Hubbard
2013 "Some emerging principles for mobile-assisted language learning". Available at: http://www.tirfonline.org/english-in-the-workforce/mobile-assisted-language- learning (date of access: 20 December 2015).

Taveira-Gomes Tiago – Rui Prado-Costa – Milton Severo – Maria Amélia Ferreira
2015 "Characterization of medical students recall of factual knowledge using learning objects and repeated testing in a novel e-learning system", BMC Med Educ. 24/15/4. Available at: doi: 10.1186/s12909-014-0275-0 (date of access: 15 November 2015).

Taylor, Robert B.
2005 *The Clinician's Guide to Medical Writing*. Berlin, Heidelberg, New York: Springer.

Traxler, John
2009 "Learning in a mobile age", *International Journal of Mobile and Blended Learning, 1*(1), 1–12.

Turula, Anna
2015 "Digital TEFL training programmes – in search of a bridge well-balanced", in Anna Turula – Maria Chojnacka (eds.), 91–110.

Turula, Anna – Maria Chojnacka
2015 *CALL for Bridges between School and Academia*. Frankfurt am Main: Peter Lang.

Vavoula, Giasemi – Norbert Pachler – Agnes Kukulska-Hulme (eds.)
2009 *Researching Mobile Learning: Frameworks, Tools and Research Designs*. Oxford: Peter Lang Verlag.

Wang Jing – Shao Liang – Guang-chun Ge
2008 "Establishment of a medical academic word list", *English for Specific Purposes, 27*, 442–58.

Wong, Lung-Hsiang – Marcelo Milrad – Marcus Specht (eds.),
2015 *Seamless Learning in the Age of Mobile Connectivity*. Berlin: Springer.

Agnieszka Gadomska
SWPS University of Social Sciences and Humanities, Warsaw, Poland

Opening the Moodle Platform to Digital Natives – Towards More Effective Motivation in the Academic Context

Abstract
The Moodle platform has been used by educators worldwide for more than ten years now. Both its programmers and users are aware of the need to constantly update it so as to meet the demands of the community, the fast changing technology and learners' expectations and needs. SWPS University is among the 79 million Moodle users. The institution trained the first group of teachers in Moodle technology in 2004. Since then the platform has been used for a variety of courses, including a large selection of Practical English blended courses offered as part of the English Studies curriculum. The article discusses the innovative method of using the Moodle platform to boost student IT skills, motivation and knowledge of the methodology of using IT in the TEFL class, the method that focuses on the learners becoming creators of Moodle content and on combining Moodle with IWB technology and TEFL methodology.

Keywords: Moodle, IWB, TEFL, user roles, teacher training, teacher authoring in CALL

1. Introduction

Moodle, short for Modular Object-Oriented Dynamic Learning Environment, as its very name specifies, is a dynamic learning platform. Moodle's success can be partially attributed to its flexibility and constant accommodation to the needs of its users. It first revolutionized education by giving teachers authoring tools, a platform for collaborative content construction and management. With the passage of time and digital natives becoming pre-service teacher trainees, however, it has had to make the authoring power available to the learners. Relying only on the assumption that "Technology used as a motivational tool encourages and engages students in learning" (Otero 2005: 12) is no longer sufficient. The "wow" factor for the digital natives is no longer being the back seat passengers of technology-driven vehicles, but rather the front seat passengers or even drivers. "Ideally, teacher students should be involved in the process of resource authoring (texts, recordings, videos, interactive quizzes, Moodle activities) in order to acquire the skills of preparing digital teaching aids" (Krajka 2014: 8).

The chapter aims at presenting how Moodle adapts to the expectations of its users, how mobile technology influences the learning process and, in effect, pre-service training, how learners influence teaching methods, what teachers who are digital immigrants can learn from their students, how the role of the teacher changes, how to enhance student and teacher motivation so that all parties understand the necessity of their active involvement in designing and implementing an effective learning management system. The above-mentioned factors are particularly important when designing teacher training programmes. By enabling teacher trainees to author IT resources and take on the role of teachers in IT-based courses, we respond not only to the needs of learners but also to the needs of teachers, who frequently profit from the expertise of digital natives. Openness to new trends, the demands of educational technology users and the fast changing teaching environment is inevitable. Giving teacher trainees the role of teachers in IT-based courses is a sign of this openness; however, it requires taking into consideration a variety of methodological, institutional, technical and financial factors.

The case study presented here is an example of good practice illustrated by the IT in TEFL course at SWPS University of Social Sciences and Humanities. There has been a strong correlation between the use of ICT and language learning. Language teachers, frequently expected to construct content, quickly realized the huge potential of the medium. However, it must be stressed that there are several factors that influence this process, including: institutional, social and professional constraints (Beaven et al. 2010). The SWPS University facilities, institutional support and teacher attitude contributed to an extensive experience in Moodle usage for tertiary level education and for pre- and in-service teacher training. IT in TEFL course participants (19 trainees in the 6th semester of their BA studies) were involved in the design and implementation of Moodle content for TEFL. For the purpose of course evaluation and its contribution to the programme of pre-service teacher training, research was conducted which included: a post-study questionnaire (plus a Moodle discussion forum), while-study discussion fora on the quality and effectiveness of each module (including the use of Moodle), informal interviews, peer teaching observation and evaluation, and Moodle login/activity reports.

2. The philosophy behind Moodle

Since the first message posted by Peter Taylor 16 years ago via his own Moodle site, this open source LMS platform has become extremely popular in educational context worldwide. In 2010 it had one million users and it had been translated into more than 100 languages, according to the Moodle official site at http://moodle.org. "The inauguration of the Moodle Research conference in 2012 served as a reminder that, however advanced the technology, Moodle design and development is guided by social constructionist pedagogy" (History. MoodleDocs 2015). Constructionism strengthens active learner participation in the process of knowledge construction, highlighting the particular effectiveness of "constructing something for others to experience" (History. MoodleDocs 2015). Piaget and Bruner showed that direct experience, including error making and search for solutions, leads to the "assimilation and accommodation of information" (Smyrnova-Trybulska 2012: 54). According to Smyrnova-Trybulska (2012: 55), in line with Piaget's theory, CLMS Moodle gives learners a unique opportunity to construct their own learning process and develop cognitive potential. Social constructivism, on the other hand, extends this principle to group context, "(…) social settings, wherein groups construct knowledge for one another, collaboratively creating a small culture of shared artifacts with shared meanings. When one is immersed within a culture like this, one is learning all the time about how to be a part of that culture, on many levels" (Philosophy. MoodleDocs 2015).

The philosophy of Moodle focuses on learning from the learner's perspective, adjusting the medium to his or her needs rather than using the medium only to publish the material *ex cathedra*. It is suggested that the role of a teacher changes from the mere knowledge provider and assessor to an "influencer," and "role model of class culture". "Consideration of these issues can help to focus on the experiences that would be best for learning from the learner's point of view, rather than just publishing and assessing the information you think they need to know. It can also help you realize how each participant in a course can be a teacher as well as a learner" (Philosophy. MoodleDocs 2015).

3. Teacher authoring as an effective policy enhancing student motivation

3.1 Moodle demotivators

For many teachers using technology in the classroom is still a challenge as they consider themselves 'technopeasants,' 'technophobes,' 'resident Luddites,' or 'stupid about computers' (Jacobsen, Clifford and Friesen 2002 as cited in Gadomska and Krajka 2015). Krajka (as cited in Gadomska and Krajka 2015) believes that teachers tend to exaggerate their computer illiteracy. Nevertheless, many teachers are confronted with their students' extensive IT competence and expectations and thus frequently resign from IT usage in the classroom, being afraid of losing face in front of their pupils (Gadomska and Krajka 2015; Chambers and Bax 2006).

Another negative factor influencing the effective usage of IT-based teaching resources in the classroom concerns students who have had long experience with e-learning, especially with self-study components. Most of the resources, especially Moodle-aided blended learning modules, tend to use repetitive, drill-based instruction. In addition, they require self-study skills and depend on learner autonomy. "Also poor quality of early CALL programs might have created a negative view of technology-enhanced teaching for many teachers, who could have experienced such 'drill-and-kill' instruction themselves as learners" (Rusiecki 1991, 1993 as cited in Gadomska and Krajka 2015).

In order to successfully confront the growing number of disillusioned and IT competent academic users of e-learning and to adjust the medium to the fast changing demands of the market, both platform providers and users should join efforts to motivate all parties involved in using IT in the educational context. The solutions in question may include: shifting the power of authoring on Moodle and combining Moodle with IWB and mobile learning tools.

3.2 Student authoring on the Moodle

One such attempt is exemplified by the changes that occurred to the *role* status and permissions of a user on the Moodle platform - very much in-line with the Moodle philosophy - which also permitted swapping the student and teacher roles in a course and, in effect, providing students with a video-game kind of experience and a virtual world where they can have hands-on experience in creating and managing e-learning content as teachers do in their own course.

The newest Moodle versions allow for assigning roles to users in different context types (Fig.1):

Figure 1. Assigning roles to users on the Moodle platform (after Standard roles. MoodeDocs 2015)

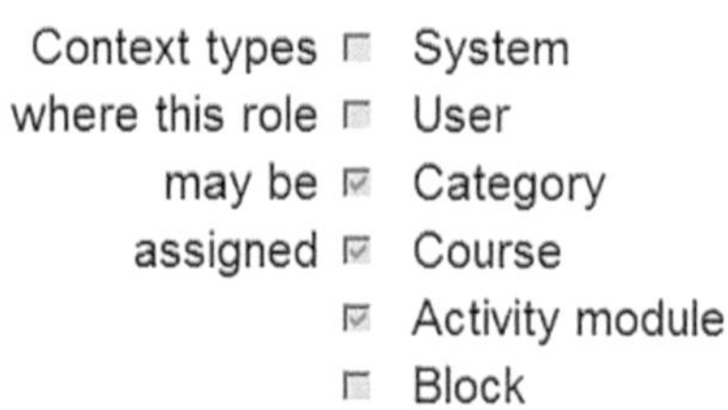

Each role has a specific range of permissions:

- *Site administrator – can "do everything" on the site*
- *Manager – a lesser administrator role*
- *Course creator – can create courses*
- *Teacher – can manage and add content to courses*
- *Non-editing teacher – can grade in courses but not edit them*
- *Student – can access and participate in courses*
- *Guest – can view courses but not participate*
- *Authenticated user – the role all logged in users have*
- *Authenticated user on the front page role – a logged in user role for the front page only*

(Standard roles. MoodleDocs 2015)

Moodle documentation materials from the official site propose giving more permissions to students. By overriding a *student* role and giving them the role of a *non-editing teacher*, we foster online peer-editing techniques, for example, we can:

1. *Give a student forum moderator rights*
   - *Enable a user to edit or delete forum posts, split discussions and move discussions to other forums*
2. *Enable a student to grade assignment submissions*
   - *A form of peer assessment/evaluation*
   - *Similar use: Enable a student to grade essay questions in a quiz*
3. *Give a student the rights to approve/ rate database module entries*
   - *Enable a user to approve, edit and delete database module entries*
   - *Similar use: Give a student the rights to approve glossary entries*
4. *Enable students to rate forum posts*

(Using Roles. Google Docs 2015)

All the above-cited permissions foster student authoring, a method that boosts student self-esteem and motivation because it gives them more freedom, assumes and involves their IT competence, and provides an authentic learning environment. The hands-on experience changes student perspective; by experiencing the limitations of the medium, students become more sensitive to teachers' objections and reactions. In terms of social competences, the users learn the netiquette, time management, copyright, and many more important issues. "By allowing students the same power and flexibility as the teacher, agency shifts so that teachers become participants in the students' activities and students become critical consumers of the teacher's activities" (Palak, 2004: 17).

3.3 Moodle's compatibility with IWB technology

Interactive whiteboards have been used in the world's classrooms for over 20 years now. Educators have discovered a huge potential of the medium despite its obvious technical or financial limitations.

> It is new generation equipment using wireless technologies. It is characterized by the high quality image and very functional software. As a result of it is considered to offer a breakthrough in use of informative technologies in teaching in many European countries... The whiteboard is not only a device used to present information in form of text, graphics, sound or animation. This is done by a computer connected to a multimedia projector. Its most important advantage is its interactive software adjusted to efficient communication between a computer and its applications and persons using it. It allows them to freely enter, manage, process and present data in a clear and effective way.
>
> (Nocny 2009).

In Poland the effectiveness of IWB-supported teaching has been under close analysis since 2004 when H. Gulińska and M. Bartoszewicz initiated their research in the Didactics of Chemistry Department of Adam Mickiewicz University in Poznań. 120 people from the middle, secondary and higher levels of education participated in the study that focused on the effectiveness of the use of IWB vs. a computer and traditional classroom instruction for teaching life sciences. Gulińska and Bartoszewicz (2007) claim that the reasons for the higher effectiveness of IWB-based teaching in middle and high schools is the possibility of modifying lesson sequences, easier restructuring and referencing to previous lesson stages or elements, attractive methods (dynamic and interactive presentations) of content explanation, etc. Moreover, IWB helps to individualize teaching by adjusting the methods and techniques to student needs and expectations. According to Gulińska and Bartoszewicz (2007), the effectiveness of a computer-room-based lesson is higher in university groups because of the students' self-study skills and learner autonomy, which are not yet fully developed at the earlier stages of education.

The most recent research on the effects of IWB technology on student achievement has been published in the report prepared by American researchers Heystead and Marzano (2012). Their respondents (K-12 teachers) claim that IWB is the most valuable digital resource in the classroom:

- 93 % say the IWB helps them be more effective;
- 83 % say it increases student motivation;
- 78 % say it stimulates student discussions;
- 75 % say it stimulates student creativity;
- 70 % say it is directly related to student achievement.

"If an experienced teacher who's been using technology for two or more years uses the board appropriately for 75 percent of the class time, and has enough training to be confident in his or her use of the technology, student achievement gains were highest" (Stansbury 2009). Heystead and Marzano (2012) agree that although teachers immediately recognize the potential value of the medium and it is often number one on their must-have list, they need sufficient training to be confident confident IWB users.

In the blended learning environment, the Moodle platform can be used with IWB technology for a variety of class activities. It can serve storing and presenting digitally mastered materials, referencing, conducting listening, speaking and writing activities, interactive practicing as well as knowledge and skill testing. Using Moodle together with the IWB tools enables more individualized and personalized teaching, i.e. meeting student needs and expectations, matching the context with students' particular learning styles, or departing from routine methods and techniques. Moreover, it boosts motivation, strengthens IT skills and media literacy, collaboration and interdisciplinary teaching (Pumilia-Gnarini 2013). "Active learning has replaced passive transmission in a multimedia context, making metacognitive learning more effective" (Pumilia-Gnarini 2013:113).

Flipped classroom is another, recently popular, educational strategy used in blended learning which can make Moodle more attractive to learners. Contrary to a traditional classroom, the content is delivered online, while what is often traditionally treated as self-study is shifted to the classroom. Therefore, more classroom time is devoted to making the content meaningful and useful, and to developing analytical and critical skills.

> We are actively transferring the responsibility and ownership of learning from the teacher to the students in a Flipped Classroom. When students have control over how they learn content, the pace of their learning, and how their learning is assessed, the learning belongs to them. Teachers become guides to understanding rather than dispensers of facts, and students become active learners rather than receptacles of information. (Bennett et al. 2013)

By retrieving information from the Moodle platform, with the use of IWB software and tools, such as a pen, spotlight, magnifier, shade, highlighter, eraser, screen capture, etc, a teacher can adjust the teaching process to his/her aims, lesson objectives and students' needs (Gadomska, Morusiewicz, Krajka 2012)

3.4 Moodle goes mobile

During the 2015 MoodleMoot US, the Moodle creator, lead developer and executive director talked about the future of Moodle, which entails such projects as: Moodle Cloud and Moodle Mobile 2.0 (Figures 2–3). He claims that Moodle develops basing on the feedback the organization receives from people, environment and testing, and reminded one of the Moodle mission statements: "Moodle allows anyone to contribute to global education" (Dougiamas 2015).

Figure 2. Moodle course content on the tablet view (after Screenshots. MoodleDocs 2015)

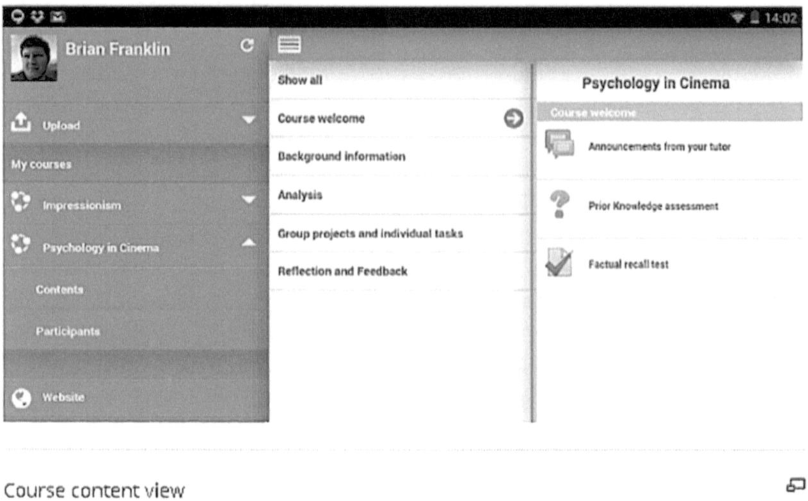

Figure 3. Moodle user tablet view (after Screenshots. MoodleDocs 2015)

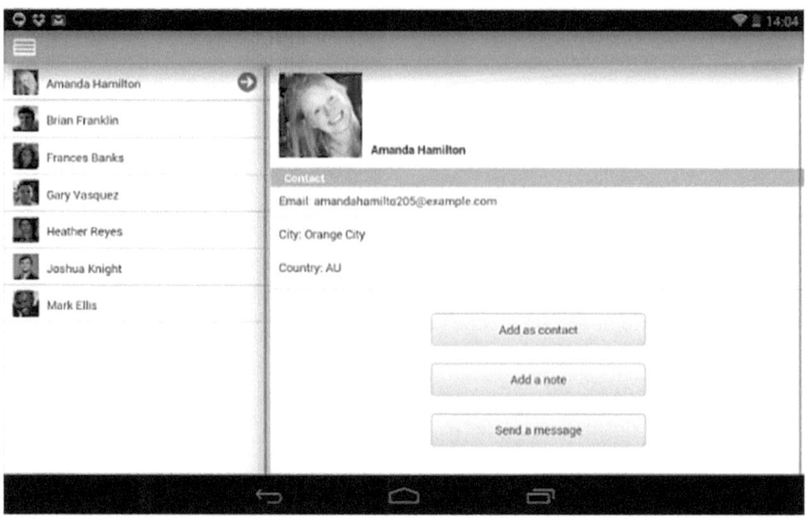

According to MoodleDocs (Screenshots, MoodleDocs 2015), the most important features of the Moodle mobile application are the following:

- *Responsive design for phones and tablets*
- *Upload a picture into your private file area*
- *Record an audio file and upload it into your private file area*
- *Send a private message to a course participant (can be done offline)*
- *Take a personal note about a course participant (can be done offline)*
- *Add a course participant to your phone contact*
- *Call a course participant touching the phone number*
- *Locate a course participant address on Google map*
- *Download and view some resources*
- *Quick access to your course contents*
- *View calendar events (require Moodle 2.5.5 or Moodle 2.6.2 and onwards)*
- *Mobile notifications (Push)*
- *Remote layout/style customization (see below)*
- *Upload any type of file from your device to your Moodle private files area*
- ** Support for sites using CAS or Shibboleth as auth methods*
- ** View calendar events*
- ** View your private messages and notifications*
- ** View your activity and course total grades in a course*
- ** Browse and download your private and course files*
- ** View forum discussions*

(Screenshots. MoodleDocs 2015)

All the above-mentioned solutions lead to more student-centred teaching. They require strong learner autonomy skills, but they also provide 24/7 access to the learning environment. While most scholars point to the benefits of using mobile technology in education, critics point to economic, ethical, curricular, technical (Baran 2014) and health concerns.

5. The case study

5.1 Aims and design

The case study concerns the SWPS University English Studies students of the 2014/15 edition of the IT in TEFL course (BA level, teaching specialization) who were, in fact, granted the role of teachers on Moodle ("Teachers can do almost anything within a course, including adding or changing the activities and grading students") as the non-editing teacher "(…) is able within a course to view and grade students' work but may not alter or delete any of the activities or resources" (Standard Roles. MoodleDocs 2015).

The aims of the course were as follows:

- ✓ to acquaint students with the use of Information and Communication technologies for the language classroom
- ✓ to gain a better understanding of a variety of aspects involved in the process of teaching English with technology
- ✓ to acquaint students with distance learning (e-learning), Interactive Whiteboard technology and methodology
- ✓ to collect a wide repertoire of ICT teaching techniques used in TEFL
- ✓ to prepare students to be able to select, adapt and create ICT-based ELT materials to suit adult learners' needs and abilities
- ✓ to provide reflective methodology tasks/case studies, referring to students' experience as ICT users and supporting their experience through an analysis of current methodological trends
- ✓ to provide students with critical and analytical skills that will help them conduct a comparative evaluation of different teaching methods and language teaching materials (IT in TEFL 2015 syllabus).

A detailed description of the course outcomes and a follow-up study may be found in Gadomska and Krakowian's "Implementing blogs for developing academic writing skills in a variety of higher educational contexts" (forthcoming).

As part of the IT in TEFL course syllabus, 18 students were asked to design their own Moodle topics/units with a variety of activities, use them as part of the blended language learning context, i.e. assign activities for self-study and class work, grade them and respond to feedback and discussion (Fig. 4). Moreover, they were required to:

- *to prepare in writing a detailed plan and description of activities for the microteaching session (45 min.) integrating traditional teaching methods and techniques with ICT tools: IWB, the Moodle platform, indicating potential problems and ways of solving them, focusing on the process of individualizing TEFL by the use of ICT tools, and providing an exercise conducted with and without the use of IT*
- *to conduct a peer-teaching activity based on their Moodle module with the use of IWB technology (15 min.)*

(IT in TEFL course syllabus)

The doors were open as to the target learner's age, his or her language competence and needs, teaching content, techniques, activities, the settings, etc. The topics included: past times, holiday destinations, global problems, intercultural aspects, etc. "[Students] really enjoyed designing their own e-material and cooperating with their colleagues as members of the community of practice. The teacher's role was to train them and supervise the work, suggesting improvements, changes and editing feedback. However, the teacher's main role was that of their immediate audience" (Gadomska and Krakowian, forthcoming). Once the course was created, it was left open throughout the semester. Therefore, the peer online teaching extended the usual class time for such an activity and was close to authentic VLE conditions, typical of hybrid courses.

Figure 4. Student module screenshot. (after: IT in TEFL online Moodle component)

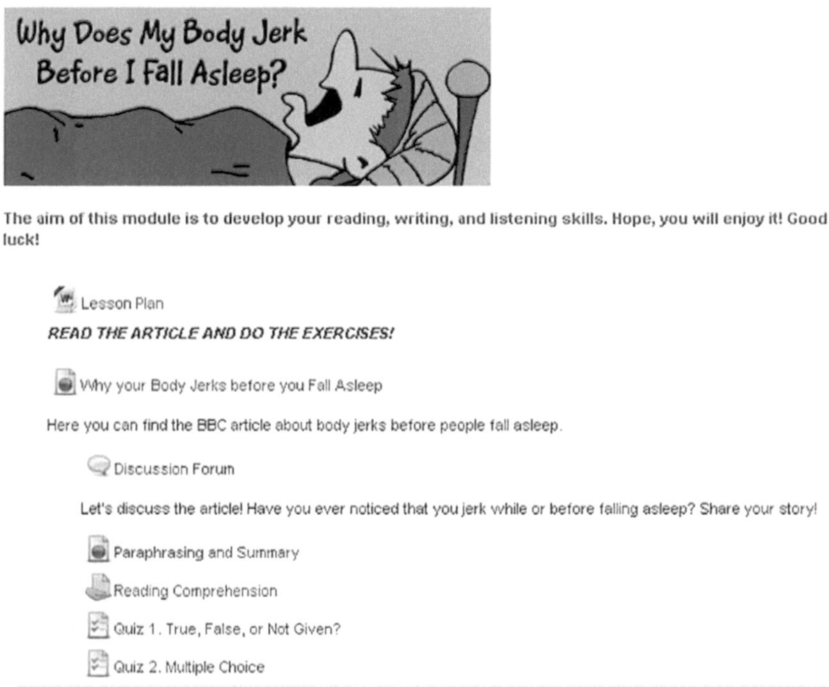

5.2 Findings

At the end of the course, the participants were asked to self-reflect on the method and this unique experience (Fig. 5) and to choose their favourite module (Fig. 6). For the latter purpose a standard Forum activity was used on the course page. The tool permitted an interactive discussion instead of a traditional questionnaire. For voting, a Choice tool was used. In both activities all the answers were viewable to all the participants, which stimulated the discussion and gave learners an impression of content transparency. Moreover, as content authors, the students were asked to provide feedback from a different perspective than in a traditional teacher/class evaluation process.

Figure 5. Self-reflection activity (after: IT in TEFL online Moodle component)

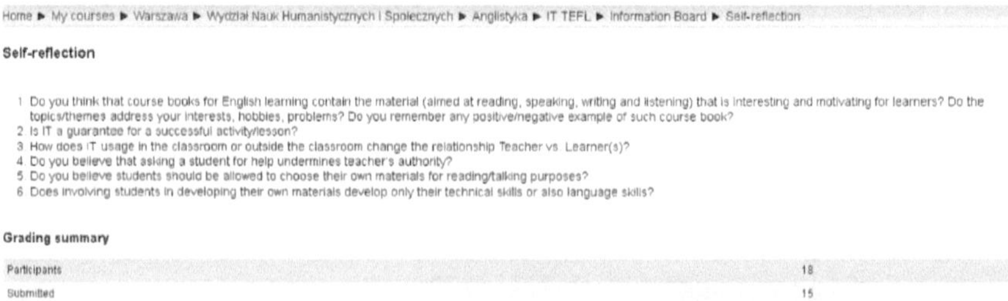

Figure 6. "Vote for the best module" activity (after: IT in TEFL online Moodle component)

The study phase involved an online questionnaire (Fig. 5) which was addressed to the users of the IT in TEFL course on both BA (15 participants) and MA levels (14 participants)[1]. The results of the study show that:

1 The results of the MA study were originally presented in Gadomska, A., and Krakowian, P., "Implementing blogs for developing academic writing skills in a variety of higher

- 16 out of 29 (8 BA and 8 MA) students believe that IT is not a guarantee of a successful lesson, while 14 out of 29 (7 BA and 6 MA) students believe it is a guarantee. Among the latter group, seven participants pointed to the usefulness of IT materials under certain conditions, especially in a blended mode. One person said that it is the quality of the materials, not the medium, that matters most. Two interviewees believe that IT should be used outside the classroom only.
- All the participants agree that IT usage for TEFL purposes changes the teacher-student relationship in a positive way; in particular, it improves communication between the teacher and learners and among learners. It should be stressed that younger students, i.e. those at BA level, see the attractiveness of IT-enhanced teaching in shortening the teacher-learner distance and providing a more relaxed and less stressful classroom atmosphere. BA students also say that IT helps avoid boredom in the classroom. On the other hand, MA students (who have some real life teaching experience) view a teacher using IT in the classroom as more professional, "cool", creative and student-friendly.
- 29 interviewees agree that asking a student for help does not undermine the teacher's authority. Three people stress the fact that it may even strengthen the teacher's position in the classroom; one respondent claims that it strengthens the teacher's self-esteem; one emphasizes that students are willing to help and that it is a normal situation. Only one person mentions the age factor, which in the case of little children may prove the opposite; one person says it all depends on the teacher-learner rapport, and another person claims that if the teacher asks for help too often, it may undermine the teacher's authority.
- 21 (9 BA and 12 MA) students agree that learners should be allowed to choose their own materials for reading/talking purposes in an EFL context. Seven students definitely see the teacher as the only materials provider. However, it should be stressed that MA students are more aware of a variety of factors influencing this decision, such as learner needs, age, aim of the activity, etc.
- All participants agree that IT usage boosts not only technical skills but also language skills.

Having designed their own Moodle modules, students were required to conduct an in-class peer teaching activity, using their own module. It was observed that Moodle-based activities are highly motivating when used in the classroom with IWB technology. Obviously, this particular course required special equipment

educational contexts", *Int. J. Continuing Engineering Education and Life-long Learning*, Vol. X, No. Y, pp. 000–000. (in the review process) and, in effect, class type distribution and planning, with the Moodle design phase classes in a computer room and peer teaching classes in the room with the IWB. The strategy proved worth the effort. Students conducted micro-teaching sessions, with the use of their self-selected Moodle activities, adjusted to the sequence objectives, learning outcomes and aims (Fig. 7). They were also asked to demonstrate an "unplugged" version of the activity, and compare and contrast the two delivery methods and techniques.

Figure 5. SWPS University student peer-teaching activity based on her own Moodle unit.

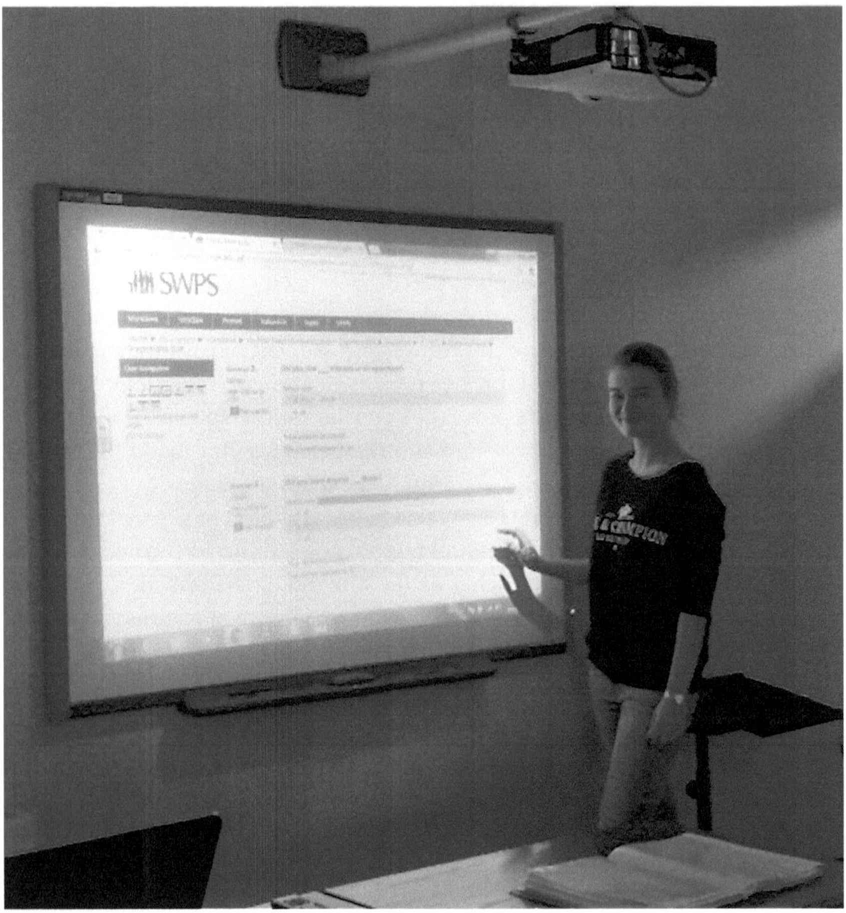

4 Conclusions

It is clearly visible that the Moodle platform is very dynamic and responsive to the needs of its users. An open source VLE is not synonymous with guaranteeing the freedom of choice - a quality cherished by educators and especially users who are digital natives. Dougiamas (2015) acknowledges in the Moodlemoot 2015 US keynote that "more developers with user experience specialization" need to be employed to develop Moodle. Like many IT-experienced educators, Moodle developers have realized that only by being open to the users' experience can program designers and educators develop successful digital solutions. The community of teachers, in turn, is directly confronted with learners' needs and expectations. Prensky (2001) in his influential text *Digital Natives, Digital Immigrants* claims:

> They [the students] have spent their entire lives surrounded by and using computers, videogames, digital music players, video cams, cell phones, and all the other toys and tools of the digital age… Our students today are all "native speakers" of the digital language of computers, video games and the Internet… Unfortunately for our Digital Immigrant teachers, the people sitting in their classes grew up on the "twitch speed" of video games and MTV. They are used to the instantaneity of hypertext, downloaded music, phones in their pockets, a library on their laptops, beamed messages and instant messaging. They've been networked most or all of their lives. They have little patience for lectures, step-by-step logic, and "tell-test" instruction. Digital Immigrant teachers assume that learners are the same as they have always been, and that the same methods that worked for the teachers when they were students will work for their students now. But that assumption is no longer valid. Today's learners are different.
>
> (Prensky 2001: 1–3)

Student authoring in CALL, although rooted in traditional teacher training methodology, is a symptom of social change, a process that involves evolution and progress. Therefore, all parties involved should do their best to contribute to effective global and local education, global by providing feedback to the IT community of designers and local by implementing innovative teaching solutions and being open in order to meet the challenges of the future.

References

2015 "Assign roles" (MoodleDocs). Available at: https://docs.moodle.org/26/en/Assign roles (date of access: 6 October 2015).

2015 "History" (MoodleDocs). Available at: https://docs.moodle.org/28/en/History (date of access: 6 October 2015).

2015 "Philosophy" (MoodleDocs). Available at: https://docs.moodle.org/28/en/Philosophy (date of access: 6 October 2015).

2015 "Screenshots" (MoodleDocs). Available at: https://docs.moodle.org/26/en/Mobile_app#Screenshots (date of access: 6 October 2015).
2015 "Standard roles" (MoodleDocs). Available at: https://docs.moodle.org/24/en/Standard roles (date of access: 6 October 2015).
2015 "Using roles" (MoodleDocs). Available at: https://docs.moodle.org/24/en/Using roles (date of access: 6 October 2015).
2015 "Efekty" Available at: http://www.edunews.pl/ (date of access: 8 August 2015).
2014/15 "*IT in TEFL* Syllabus." SWPS University
2015 "Początki" Available at: http://www.edunews.pl/ (date of access: 8 August 2015).
[n.d.] „Początki tablicy interaktywnej Interwrite." (n.d.). Available at: http://www.interwrite.pl/?menu=rozwiazania&main=solutionDet&solID=74&tab=-1 (date of access 8 August 2015).
2013/14 "Testing e-Learning," University SWPS [online] Available at: www.swps.edu.pl (date of access 8 October 2015).

Baran, Evrim
2014 "A review of research on mobile learning in teacher education", *Educational Technology & Society 17*(4), 17–32. Available at: http://www.ifets.info/journals/17_4/2.pdf (date of access: 02 January 2016).

Beaven, Tita (ed.)
2010 "Needs and challenges for online language teachers – the ECML project DOTS". *Teaching English with Technology: A Journal for Teachers of English 10*(2), 5–20.

Bennett Brian - Dan Spencer - Jon Bergmann - Troy Cockrum - Ramsey Musallam - Aaron Sams - Karl Fisch - Jerry Overmyer
2013 " The Flipped Class Manifest". The Daily Riff – BE SMARTER. ABOUT EDUCATION. (n.d.). Available at: http://www.thedailyriff.com/articles/the-flipped-class-manifest-823.php (date of access: 02 January 2016).

Chambers, Angela - Stephen Bax
2006 "Making CALL work: Towards normalisation". System, *34*, 2006, 465–479.

Dougiamas Martin
2015 "The future of Moodle" Keynote U.S MoodleMoot 2015. Available at: https://www.youtube.com/watch?v=8-e7_eqbNnQ (date of access 10 November 2015).

Gadomska, Agnieszka - Rafał Morusiewicz - Jarosław Krajka
2012 "Kształtowanie kompetencji kluczowych w e-learningu jako sposób na indywidualizację nauczania języka obcego", in Jolanta Knieja – Sebastian Piotrowski (eds.), 425–441.

Gadomska, Agnieszka – Jarosław Krajka
2015 "Pedagogical solutions in e-teacher training. Towards effective technology adoption by teachers", in Eugenia Smyrnova-Trybulska (ed.), 297–312.

Gadomska, Agnieszka - Przemysław Krakowian
[forthcoming] "Implementing blogs for developing academic writing skills in a variety of higher educational contexts", *Int. J. Continuing Engineering Education and Life-long Learning, X*(Y), 000–000.

Gnarini Paolo
2013 *Handbook of Research on Didactic Strategies and Technologies for Education: Incorporating Advancements.* Hershey, PA: Information Science Reference.
"Moodle: a platform for the schools". Available at: (https://www.youtube.com/watch?v=8-e7_eqbNnQ (date of access 8 November 2015).

Gulińska, Hanna - Malgorzata Bartoszewicz
2007 „Tablica interaktywna środkiem wspomagającym nauczanie." *E-mentor 1*(18). Available at: http://www.e-mentor.edu.pl/artykul/indcx/numer/18/id/383 (date of access: 8 August 2015).

Guzdial Mark
1999 "Teacher and student authoring on the Web for shifting agency" *Proceedings of AERA 1999.* Available at: http://guzdial.cc.gatech.edu/papers/aera99/default.html (date of access: 02 January 2016).

Haystead, Mark W. - Robert J. Marzano
2012 *Executive Summary: A Randomized Controlled Trial of the Effects of Promethean ActivExpression on Student Achievement.* Centennial, CO: Marzano Research Laboratory, Available at: http://www.prometheanworld.com/rx_content/files/PDF/MarzanoTrialoftheEffectsofPrometheanActivExpressiononStudentAchievement-171115.pdf (date of access: 8 August 2015).

Kessler, Greg – Lia Plakans
2008 "Does teachers' confidence with CALL equal innovative and integrative use?", *Computer Assisted Language Learning, 21*(3), 269–282.

Krajka, Jarosław
2012 *The Language Teacher in the Digital Age – Towards a Systematic Approach to Digital Teacher Development,* Lublin: Wydawnictwo UMCS.

Krajka, Jarosław
2014 "Student teachers and teacher students. Telecollaboration in LSP teacher education" *English for Specific Purposes World, 43*(15), 1–9. Available at: http://www.esp-world.info/Articles_43/Krajka.pdf. (date of access: 02 January 2016).

Nocny, Magdalena
2009 "Place of the interactive whiteboard in higher education of the Polish educational system." In *Celebrating geographical diversity: Proceedings of the HERODOT Conference in Ayvalik, Turkey, 28–30 May 2009*. Berlin: Mensch und Buch Verlag, Available at: http://www.herodot.net/conferences/ayvalik/papers/educ-13.pdf (date of access 8 August 2015).

Otero, Valerie
2005 "Integrating technology into teacher education: A critical framework for implementing reform". *Journal of Teacher Education, 56*(1), 8–23. Available at: https://petechnologypet673.wikispaces.com/file/view/Otero%20%282005%29%20Integrating%20T%20into%20Teacher%20Education.pdf/434420700/Otero%20%282005%29%20Integrating%20T%20into%20Teacher%20Education.pdf. (date of access: 02 January 2016).

Palak, Deniz
2004 "Design strategies for higher education faculty." *The Turkish Online Journal of Educational Technology, 3*(3), 11–23.

Prensky, Mark
2001 "Digital natives, digital immigrants" *On the Horizon, 9*(5). Available at: http://www.marcprensky.com/writing/Prensky%20-%20Digital%20Natives,%20Digital%20Immigrants%20-%20Part1.pdf (date of access: 11 November 2015).

Prensky, Mark
[n.d.] "Digital natives, digital immigrants part 2: Do they really think differently?" *On the Horizon,* 1–6. Available at: http://www.marcprensky.com/writing/Prensky - Digital Natives, Digital Immigrants - Part1.pdf (date of access: 11 November 2015).

Stansbury, Meris
2009 "SETDA forum illuminates key ed-tech trends." *eSchool News. Daily Tech news and Innovation*. Available at: http://www.eschoolnews.com/2009/11/04/setda-forum-illuminates-key-ed-tech-trends/ (date of access 14 May 2015).

Warschauer, Mark - Lonnie Turbee - Bruce Roberts
1996 "Computer learning networks and student empowerment." *System, 14*(1), 1–14.

Elżbieta Gajek
Institute of Applied Linguistics, University of Warsaw, Warsaw, Poland

Translation Revisited in Audiovisual Teaching and Learning Contexts on the Example of Clipflair Project

Abstract
Translation has been widely used in foreign language methodology. However, its use is still controversial. Digital technology adds new dimensions to using translation tasks, both to teaching techniques and methodology, as it permits the use of audiovisual materials as stimuli for learning activities and as end products. Technology not only facilitates the use of audiovisual materials but also enables the introduction of new tasks involving the use of captioning and revoicing. Captioning refers mainly to subtitling. Revoicing covers dubbing, voiceover, audio description, narration and commentaries (Pérez-González 2009). Although audiovisual translation (AVT) originated in the 80's of the previous century, editing oral and written translated texts adds extra practice for language learners, providing them with a clear situational context. It opens new perspectives in learning and teaching languages, especially within the use of materials, strategies, social interaction and integration, assessment and curriculum issues. The paper presents interests in AVT reflected in European-Union-funded projects, and especially the role of translation with the use of technology in language learning on the basis of ClipFlair methodological solutions. The shift from monosemiotic translation to intersemiotic translation for language learning purposes in a technologically rich environment opens a new area for research and teaching practice.

Keywords: learning and teaching languages, audiovisual materials, translation, subtitling, audio description, revoicing

1. Introduction

Although translation as a technique in teaching and learning languages has been widely discussed for decades (Cook 2010), it is now gaining a new dimension. Advancement in digital technology makes it possible for learners and teachers to use rendering in an audiovisual context; that is audiovisual texts with ready-made professional interlingual or intralingual translations have become learning materials. They are also source texts for translation. The results of students' translation can be stored alongside with the audiovisual text in the form of captioning, which involves subtitling, and revoicing, i.e. dubbing, voice over, audio description, narrating and commentaries. As audiovisual materials for learning FL are widely accessible in digital environments, the technology has opened new dimensions of FL methodology. This encouraged the development of methodological and practical solutions which have been implemented in the ClipFlair project.

The aim of the article is to reflect on the role of translation in foreing language learning and teaching in the light of the intersemiotic aspects of interaction with audiovisual texts.

2. Review of literature

Audiovisual Translation (AVT) for language learning is well grounded in literature as it refers to: (1) the role of translation in teaching languages; (2) the place of audiovisual materials in language learning; (3) the effects of captioning on learning outcomes; (4) the techniques of revoicing for learning; and (5) the role of technology in AVT learning tasks.

2.1. Translation in foreign language teaching and learning

The usefulness of translation for language learning has been discussed for years (Cook 2010). In the past mainly disadvantages of the use of translation in language learning and teaching were listed (Duff 1992) as years ago translation, focused on monosemiotic texts, developed only reading and writing. Most of the drawbacks of such translation are overcome by widely accessible audiovisual texts. Klaudy (2003) distinguishes between *pedagogical* and *real* translation. In the former translation is a means of language acquisition, whereas in the latter it is an end in itself. Thus, Incalcaterra McLoughlin and Lertola (2014: 71) claim that "current debates, therefore, no longer concentrate on whether or not translation has a place in FL teaching. The issue is, rather, how pedagogical translation should be incorporated in the syllabus, which types of translation (monosemiotic, written, polysemiotic, multimedial) are more suitable to specific levels of fluency, which aspects of language acquisition benefit most from translation practice (lexicon, grammar, syntax) and which abilities can be enhanced through its use."

2.2. Audiovisual translation in teaching and learning

Audiovisual materials provide learners with linguistic input in clear cultural contexts. As the frequency of input plays an important role in the acquisition of linguistic items (Ellis 2003), digital audiovisual materials create an environment which enhances learning. In subtitling countries frequent exposure to linguistic input in foreign languages has become anecdotal (Danan 2004), and in countries such as Slovenia, Romania or Sweden, the media have contributed to high levels of average language proficiency, particularly among the youth. The level of language acquisition in dubbing and subtitling countries has been discussed by numerous authors, including Dollerup (1974), d'Ydewalle and Pavakanun (1997), Díaz Cintas (2003), Gottlieb (1998), and Caimi (2008). At the same time, in Spain, which is traditionally a dubbing country (Díaz Cintas 2003), this translation choice seems to be one of the main reasons behind the apparently low level of foreign language proficiency among its people (Talaván 2010). Poland, as a voiceover and dubbing country, seems to confirm the pattern, and the level of proficiency in English and German there is not satisfactory (First European Survey of Language Proficiency; Final Report 2012).

Apart from enriching language teaching and learning techniques, video projects involving AVT can also contribute to a variety of assessment techniques as they allow for the holistic evaluation of skills and competences such as language and communication skills, visual literacy, cultural awareness, intercultural and media competences. They also make students aware of the importance of non-verbal and paralinguistic communication (Gajek 2011).

2.3. Captioning

Talaván (2010) makes a distinction between subtitling as support and subtitling as a task. In the former learners use ready-made interlingual or intralingual subtitles. In the latter they create their own subtitles. She emphasizes the role of authentic videos. "Subtitles and subtitling within this setting turn into very efficient tools when used to enhance foreign language education in general and oral and reading comprehension in particular, since they allow students to monitor the input, making it truly comprehensible" (Talaván 2010: 288). Gajek (2008) emphasizes the need for subtitling activities in teacher training programmes to make student teachers aware of the benefits and prepare them for effective use of AVT in their teaching practice.

2.3.1. Reception of the subtitled audiovisual input

While watching subtitled material learners are provided with three sources of linguistic input: (1) oral verbal in L2; (2) written verbal in L1; and (3) non-verbal, conveyed through images which place the language in a clear context (Ghia 2012). The visual component helps to understand what is omitted in the verbal dialogue (Tomaszkiewicz 2009)

Learners are able to acquire information from the three sources (Ghia 2012) as the message is transmitted through different communication channels. Viewers are simultaneously able to attend to the soundtrack while reading the subtitles (d'Ydewalle and Pavakanun 1996, 1997; Van de Poel and d'Ydewalle 2001), and can easily switch attention between the two (d'Ydewalle et al. 1987). At the same time, they are capable of looking at the images appearing on screen (Danan 2004).

Ghia (2012) claims that audiovisual input, enhanced with different types of subtitles, has an impact on the acquisition of various L2 skills by learners at different proficiency levels (see also: Vanderplank 1990; d'Ydewalle and Pavakanun 1996, 1997). Results showed an overall positive effect of exposure on vocabulary learning (d'Ydewalle and Pavakanun 1996, 1997; Van de Poel and d'Ydewalle 2001) and the development of listening comprehension skills in L2 (Markham and Peter 2002). Subtitling also enhances listening and speaking in beginners (Araújo 2008).

2.3.2. Learner subtitling

Subtitling as a task is an interactive and engaging activity for students, who play a very active role getting a semi-professional result which they can share with colleagues, teachers or with a wider public online. This refers to 'funsubbing' (Díaz Cintas and Muñoz Sánchez 2006), whereby people create their own subtitles and upload them to the Internet so that they can be shown together with a particular video clip. Some repositories of knowledge such as KhanAcademy and Ted.com also ask users to provide subtitles for the clips.

A subtitling task has to be carefully prepared by the teacher to facilitate learning outcomes as "the goal is not to turn foreign language students into subtitlers, but rather to use these audiovisual translation applications for didactic ends" (Talaván 2010: 289). The preparation involves a selection of user-friendly software – preferably freeware – to reduce technical problems and focus learners on the learning processes and benefits.

Talaván (2010) shows that subtitling tasks improve oral comprehension within a multimedia environment. In conclusion she claims that "Not using this type of technology to improve foreign languages in general, and English in particular, could be seen as a real waste of resources" (Talaván 2010: 295).

2.4. Revoicing

Revoicing is inter-semiotic translation which covers dubbing, voiceover, audio description, narration and commentaries (Pérez-González 2009). Below the focus will be put on audio description as a technique which involves keeping the balance between the original audiovisual text and the verbal input either received or produced by the user of the text. Audio description is also the second practical area, besides subtitling, undertaken in the ClipFlair project (see part 3 of this chapter).

Language learners receive linguistic input while they watch sports events commented, nature films, instructions on how to cook, play a game or exercise, etc. Repositories of knowledge such as KhanAcademy, Ted.com, among others, provide scientific content revoiced. Learners are exposed to the language in an engaging context, which facilitates memorization according to the input hypothesis. This also opens the teaching content to new areas, which is CLIL (Content and Language Integrated Learning).

2.4.1. Audio description

Audio description is a special type of revoicing addressed to visually impaired viewers which is supposed to enable them to acquire visual information through a verbal description attached to a clip as a separate soundtrack. Standards of audio description for the blind define clearly the style of the language. Although the standards are mainly used as guidelines for preparing audio describers for the blind, a teacher can obtain the knowledge of the rules addressed to professionals. Szymańska and Strzymiński (2010: 22) suggest "three golden rules of audio description":

- Describe what you see in the image;
- Do not interpret, do not present your conclusions, opinions or motives of actions described;
- Do not talk during the dialogue (except for the very significant actions taking place in the background).

It is not possible to describe in words everything that is visible on the screen in a very limited time. An audio describer continually selects elements of the visual content to respond to the needs of the blind (Szymańska and Strzymiński 2010). However, the use of audio description for pedagogical purposes aims at achieving language learning outcomes, not transforming learners into professional audio describers. Similarly to subtitling, adding an extra soundtrack requires user-friendly software in order to reduce the technical issues and to focus learners' attention on the linguistic aspects of the task. Learners need to familiarize themselves with the standards of audio description for the blind; however, for learning purposes they are not limited to the AD rules.

Exercises used by Sadowska (2014) to train professional audio describers can be also used in a language class as, in fact, they are rooted in language learning and teaching techniques. In order to clarify the meaning of AD Sadowska proposes watching a movie three times. The first time without image and without AD; the second time without image, but with AD; and the third time with both image and AD. This sequence is an introduction to language exercises. After the first viewing students try to guess the details of the stock, e.g. the setting, content and characters. Discussing their assumptions, they can pose questions and state what they would like to see. During the second viewing – still without image - students learn about the role of AD in explaining the content of the film. The third viewing allows full reception of the video content, reinforced by AD. Apart from the linguistic benefits, this set of exercises adds to integration – students experience the sensations received by the blind. They are prepared to play the role of audio describers. The implementation of the tasks with AD allows for modification and integration of well-known, previously used language, which mainly serves the development of speaking but also listening, writing and reading skills. Walczak (2013) presents promising results of research in the use of AD in the teaching of English to the blind and visually-impaired children.

2.4.2. Learner revoicing

Learners may revoice various texts according to their interests and needs, e.g. scientific experiments filmed at science lessons, instructions on how to perform a traditional dance. They do it in school exchange projects such as eTwinning. To make the learning environment more open to the out-of-class stimuli they may take photos or make films outside the classroom with their mobile devices, e.g. on their way to school, during a school trip, at home, and then revoice the visual materials. Beginners may start by adding a single word e.g. the name of the object, to the screen. With growing proficiency the learners' linguistic output will become more and more advanced.

3. Projects in audiovisual translation for language learning

Interest in audiovisual translation is reflected in the number of projects in AVT supported by the European Union. For example eCoLoRe, eCoLoTrain and eCoLoMedia were focused on training translation students. Others, like LeViS and ClipFlair, were focused on language learning with the use of AVT.

The Learning via Subtitles (LeViS) project was realised by a consortium of seven European universities in 2006–2008. LeViS developed a range of task-based activities for language learning in which multimedia were the central part, not the marginal one. The consortium produced a subtitling simulator LvS, which allows learners to actively participate in real-life communication while creating and adding subtitles to audiovisual material. The evaluation of the project results shows that it was well received by both learners and teachers. The activities proved to be beneficial for learners at various levels and the subtitling tool was perceived as useful for language learning (Sokoli et al. 2011; Incalcaterra McLoughlin and Lertola 2015).

3.1. ClipFlair project

ClipFlair builds on the developments and achievements of its predecessor, Learning via Subtitling (LeViS), whose innovative nature proved to motivate learners in a number of different settings, both formal and informal. ClipFlair not only provides subtitling-based activities, as LeViS did, but also involves revoicing (i.e. dubbing, voiceover, audio description, etc.) as a language learning method.

ClipFlair (*Foreign Language Learning through Interactive Captioning and Revoicing of Clips*) is an EU-financed project aimed at providing teachers and learners with a free online platform with activities facilitating foreign language learning through revoicing and captioning.

ClipFlair users are offered a freely available tool, ClipFlair Studio (http://studio.clipflair.net/), which operates both online and offline, with ready-to-use subtitling and revoicing activities at levels ranging from A1 to C2. It can be used by both students and teachers in the classroom and by individual learners in non-institutionalised settings.

In terms of methodology, ClipFlair establishes a new framework for foreign language learning rooted in the student's interaction with text, both in the written and spoken form; image, both still and moving; and sound. On top of covering the four skills traditionally recognised in language learning methodology, that is reading, listening, writing and speaking, ClipFlair develops other skills specifically related to interaction with audiovisual texts such as AV-reading, AV-speaking, AV-listening, AV-watching and AV-writing (Zabalbeascoa et al. 2012).

3.1.1. ClipFlair tasks

The Polish team (Gajek, Szarkowska 2012, 2015a, 2015b) prepared activities for learners of Polish and English. They refer to a variety of topics. The first group of tasks is addressed to learners of Polish and involves the Polish customs and traditions. The second group aims at learners of English at various levels from A1 to C2. Within this group a special subgroup is based on KhanAcademy videos to encourage teachers and learners to use repositories of knowledge as materials for language learning. Another subgroup encourages the use of the AVT tasks with small children and beginners. There are tasks with captioning and revoicing.

3.1.2. ClipFlair outcomes

Numerous ClipFlair outcomes are presented at http://clipflair.net/outcomes/ in various documents and slideshares. Among others, in the course of the project a resource library containing over 300 activities for all CEFR levels for the 15 languages targeted, accompanied by corresponding lesson plans and relevant metadata and available at http://clipflair.net, was prepared. The activities were prepared, tested and used by a community of 1500 students and teachers. The outcomes are disseminated in the project member countries and beyond, in various languages at conferences, workshops, as well as in academic and professional publications. The project reached a huge dissemination in the social media; it was estimated that in July 2014 1,204,997 people were reached only through Twitter accounts.

3.2. Students' participation in the project work – the Polish experience

Over 500 Polish students participated in the project at each stage of its development. Firstly, they created clips uploaded to the project platform. Some of the films were selected for the platform. Secondly, they used the activities at the pilot stage. Their role was to choose three activities available on the platform and evaluate them from the perspective of a learner, mainly an advanced learner of English or a beginner or intermediate learner of other languages. They could also look at the activities of their choice from the perspective of a target language teacher. Thirdly, they evaluated the final results at the dissemination phase. They uploaded a detailed evaluation of one or two selected activities on the internal project forum to make the response visible to the creators of the activity. The evaluation at both stages was descriptive. They presented their opinions on selected clips. For them the content of the clip was essential; if they liked the clip, their evaluation was positive, e.g. "The video is a good combination of the visual content and the language, as each step shown is also briefly, yet understandably described"; "I think the clip is good for language learning, because it has a simple form and is easily comprehensible one way or another"; "I like the video because it's visually appealing, the images are eye-catching, which in combination with the text read out by the speaker creates a powerful message. The video explores a very important and current topic". If the content was beyond their interest, the evaluation was neutral or critical. One student's commentary on a revoiced clip with a culinary recipe was: "I must say that the activity is brilliant" but another wrote: "this video is just a narration resembling a University lecture", which was not a complement in this context. Their perception was determined by the content. For example, the clip *Rosetta Stone* was evaluated in class in the form of focus group interviews. The students presented balanced opinions. On the one hand, they appreciated the interactivity of the tasks, and the clear and natural context of language learning, e.g. a visit to the museum in the *Rosetta Stone* video; on the other hand, they noticed the gap between the time pupils get to know about the Rosetta Stone at school and their language level, which is not high enough for them to understand the text with ease.

3.3. Students' attitudes towards the concept

The learning success depends, among others, on affective factors such as students' attitudes to the materials and tasks being used. In the evaluation surveys students expressed their opinions, e.g. "Adding narration to a video clip is a great way to stimulate creative thinking"; "It is a great addition to traditional teaching materials"; or "Extremely beneficial to students as it develops their language skills". These together with a commentary written by a student: "long, I could not be persuaded to do this task, but when we got to the resources offered to ClipFlair, I could not get away from them" testify to the attractiveness of the project materials and exercises.

Students at this stage of their professional development could evaluate the materials from both the learners' and teacher's perspective, and it turned out that the perspectives differ. As students, they were positive about the idea of using audiovisual materials by adding captioning and revoicing and they stressed the role of interlingual translation in learning through audiovisual materials. However, as teachers, they would recommend the materials to pupils for individual work at home, e.g. "Weaker students can compensate by looking at the visual material as it can help to understand what is being said", but in class they would use them only on condition that they had easy access to computers, which is unlikely, and if their pupils were computer literate enough to focus on the language task. However, they could also perceive the activity as relevant for whole class teaching in small classes, as illustrated by this quotation: "I find the video appropriate for English teaching and very flexible when it comes to the class organization and planning".

However, there are also critical voices which express controversies about the usefulness of activities based on translation to beginners. Students found such activities beneficial for advanced learners interested in translation, not for learners at lower levels of proficiency.

3.4. Openness as a feature of audiovisual digital learning environments

3.4.1. Openness in audiovisual language learning contexts

The broad concept of openness in educational contexts may refer to teachers and students' attitudes to change in their perceptions of language learning, their habits and routines. Both positive and negative aspects of educational change need to be acknowledged. On the one hand, "change means replacing an established or dominant paradigm with something new or different in order to improve the situation" (Lamie 2005: 6). On the other hand, change is viewed as a "(…) negative force incurring resistance, concern and even dread and fear" (Lamie 2005: 4) because it may involve loss of power and position. As change is inevitable – every day both teachers and learners are different, e.g. older, more experienced, more knowledgeable – the implementation of change requires training and practice. Positive attitude to change leads to its implementation as it involves awareness of innovation. A person with developed awareness of innovation should:

- "believe that the changes make sense and are possible, even on a large scale;
- have a willingness to take risks;
- determination;
- optimism;
- ability to work together;
- be able to cope with adversity;
- should also stimulate others to inspire innovative initiatives in the place they live and work." (Werner 2010: 432).

Using audiovisual texts in translation-based tasks for language learning allows for change and innovation in the following areas: materials and aids; learning and teaching strategies; curriculum integration; social relations; and learner competences.

New learning materials and tools which are widely and easily available on the Internet are used in class, which widens the opportunity to use authentic materials. Any video material, either produced for non-educational purpose or home made by the teacher and learners, can be a source for language learning tasks. Fragments of feature films or clips from repositories of knowledge may be adjusted to learners' interests and needs.

The change in teaching tools involves user-friendly online and offline instruments for revoicing and captioning. They may become language teaching tools as they do not focus students' attention on themselves but create an attractive environment for learning.

Learning strategies shift from decontextualized use of words or phrases to situations well grounded in contexts rich in cultural information and visual clues. This resembles language learning in a natural environment. Language learning strategies acquired in class may encourage students to use them outside the classroom, e.g. while they watch films for pleasure, and that creates an informal learning environment.

Teaching strategies which involve the use of AVT in language learning and teaching trigger professional creativity in teacher practitioners at any level of students' proficiency.

Curriculum integration takes place through the use of repositories of knowledge, such as KhanAcademy and TedEdu.com (Gajek and Szarkowska 2015a; Gajek and Szarkowska 2015b), or the subtitling or revoicing of home-made videorecordings of experiments or observations performed at science lessons. This opens the door to holistic learning as introduced within Content and Language Integrated Leaning (CLIL).

Social relations are widened through the use of AVT for language learning. The class is either more open to the needs of impaired learners or to international cooperation. Social integration of the blind and deaf is a result of preparing subtitles and audio description, simply by learning about the needs of both groups and doing tasks whose results can be relevant for either group. What is more, it encourages inclusive education. International collaboration takes place through collaborative projects, such as eTwinning, where students prepare visual materials for their partners and then revoice or subtitle them in the main language of cooperation within the project. Another form of international collaboration is voluntary work for repositories of knowledge, such as KhanAcademy, TedEdu.com, where learners participate in the community of practice, subtitle instructional clips to make them accessible for people who do not know the language spoken in the clip.

Last but not least, learner non-linguistic competences are being developed as intersemiotic translation contributes to the development of various skills, e.g. visual literacy, in learners.

3.4.2. The role of technology in teaching and learning with AV materials, as illustrated by the ClipFlair project

The generic role of Information and Communication Technologies (ICT) is to provide storage, access and enable communication. As exemplified by the functionalities of the ClipFlair platform, the specific role of technology is to create a safe FL learning and teaching environment to:

- provide space for storing various kinds of AV materials;
- provide tools for adding and editing written texts, audio files and pictures;
- encourage the use of combination of verbal and visual materials for language learning;
- encourage interaction with verbal and non-verbal input that enhances language learning;
- provide teachers with authoring tools for creating own teaching and learning tasks;
- allow for flexibility in sharing materials and tasks – they may or may not be displayed online;
- allow for learner and teacher autonomy as they choose topics of interest;
- enhance online communication between the teacher and learners;
- train teachers how to incorporate AVT into FL methodology;
- train learners how to enhance FL learning through AVT outside the class.

Thus, technology is not only a tool or a storage place but it is a trigger of change in language teaching and learning methodology.

4. Conclusions

The change from monosemiotic translation, developing mainly reading and writing skills, to intersemiotic translation, involving still pictures and video clips opens new dimensions into various aspects of learning and teaching languages, such as materials, strategies and assessment. But for language learners, who have nowadays access to a multitude of audiovisual materials, the most essential aspect of the clip is its content; they get involved in various language learning activities suggested by the teacher if they find the content appealing.

International cooperation in EU-funded projects on the use of AVT in class and for language learning purposes contributes to openness in terms of methodology, in search of theoretical and practical solutions, educationally sound concepts and learning tasks. The role of technology is to create a learning environment in which students acquire the target language. What is more, the learning skills which they practice while using AVT can be transferred to long-lasting learning in informal environments rich in multilingual audiovisual texts.

References

Alderete-Diez, Pilar – Laura Incalcaterra McLoughlin – Labhaoise NiDhonnchadha – Dorothy NiUigin (eds.)

2012 *Translation, Technology and Autonomy in Language Teaching and Learning*. Bern, Switzerland: Peter Lang.

Baker, Mona – Gabriela Saldanha (eds.)

2009 *The Routledge Encyclopedia of Translation Studies*. London & New York: Routledge, 2009.

Białoń, Lidia (ed.)

2010 *Zarządzanie działalnością innowacyjną*. Warszawa: Placet.

Cook, Guy

2010 *Translation in Language Teaching*. Oxford: Oxford University Press.

Danan, Martine

1992 "Reversed subtitling and dual coding theory: New directions in foreign language instruction", *Language Learning: A Journal of Applied Linguistics*, *42*(4), 497–527.

2004 "Captioning and subtitling: Undervalued language learning strategies", *META*, *49*(1), 67–77.

Díaz Cintas Jorge (ed.)

2008 *The Didactics of Audiovisual Translation*, Amsterdam/Philadelphia: John Benjamins.

Díaz Cintas, Jorge – Marco Fernandez Cruz

2008 "Using subtitled video materials for foreign language instruction", in Jorge Diaz Cintas (ed.), 201–214.

Díaz Cintas, Jorge – Anna Matamala – Joselia Neves (eds.)

2010 *New Insights into Audiovisual Translation and Media Accessibility*. Amsterdam: Rodopi.

Doughty, Catherine J. – Michal H. Long (eds.)

2003 *The Handbook of Second Language Acquisition*. Malden: Blackwell Publishing.

Duff, Alan

1992 *Translation*. Oxford: Oxford University Press.

Duszak, Anna – Anna Jopek-Bosiacka – Grzegorz Kowalski (eds.)

2015 *Tekst naukowy i jego przekład*. Kraków: Universitas.

Duszak, Anna – Grzegorz Kowalski (eds.)

2015 *Academic (Inter)genres: between Texts, Contexts and Identities*. Frankfurt am Main: Peter Lang.

d'Ydewalle, Géry – Ubolwanna Pavakanun
1997 "Could enjoying a movie lead to language acquisition?", in Peter Winterhoff-Spurk - Tom H.A. van der Voort, (eds.), 145–55.
1996 « Le sous-titrage à la télévision facilite-t-il l'apprentissage des langues ? », in Yves Gambier (ed.), 217–23.

d'Ydewalle, Géry – Johan Van Rensbergen – Joris Pollet (eds.)
1987 "Reding a message when the same message is available auditorily in another language: The case of subtitling," in John Kevin O'Regan - Ariane Lévy-Schoen (eds.), 313–21.

Ellis, Nick C.
2003 "Constructions, chunking and connectionism", in Catherine J. Doughty – Michael H. Long (eds.), 63–103.

European Commission
2013 *First European Survey of Language Proficiency*. Available at: http://ec.europa.eu/languages/policy/strategic-framework/documents/language-survey-final-report_en.pdf (date of access: 26 September 2015)

Freddi, Maria – Maria Pavesi (eds.)
2009 *Analysing Audiovisual Dialogue. Linguistic and Translational Insights*. Bologna: CLUEB.

Gajek, Elżbieta
2008 „Edukacyjne znaczenie napisów w tekście audiowizualnym" *Przekładaniec, 1*(20). 106–114.

Gajek, Elżbieta
2011 "Learner-oriented teaching and assessment through digital video projects", in Hanna Komorowska (ed.), 287–306.

Gajek, Elżbieta – Agnieszka Szarkowska
2012 "Audiodeskrypcja i napisy jako techniki uczenia się języka – projekt ClipFlair." *Języki obce w szkole, 2*, 106–110.

Gajek, Elżbieta – Agnieszka Szarkowska
2015a "Audiovisual scientific text for self-directed Content and Language Integrated Learning (CLIL)", in Anna Duszak - Grzegorz Kowalski (eds.).

Gajek, Elżbieta – Agnieszka Szarkowska
2015b „Przekład audiowizualny w edukacji językowej – na przykładzie materiałów naukowych w projekcie ClipFlair", in Anna Duszak - Anna Jopek-Bosiacka - Grzegorz Kowalski (eds.), 243–268.

Gambier, Yves (ed.)
1996 *Les Transferts Linguistiques dans les Médias Audiovisuels*. Villeneuve d'Ascq: Presses Universitaires du Septentrion.

Gambier, Yves – Henrik Gottlieb (eds.)
2001 *(Multi)Media Translation. Concepts, Practices, and Research.* Amsterdam: Benjamins.

Ghia, Elisa
2012 "Audiovisual translation as acquisitional input: Quantitative and qualitative aspects," in Pilar Alderete-Diez - Laura Incalcaterra McLoughlin – Labhaoise NiDhonnchadha - Dorothy NiUigin (eds.), 117–136.

Incalcaterra McLoughlin, Laura – Marie Biscio – Márie Á. Ní Mhainnín (eds.)
2011 *Audiovisual Translation Subtitles and Subtitling Theory and Practice.* Bern: Peter Lang.

Incalcaterra McLoughlin, Laura – Jennifer Lertola
2014 "Audiovisual translation in second language acquisition. Integrating subtitling in the foreign-language curriculum", *The Interpreter and Translator Trainer, 8*(1), 70–83, DOI: 10.1080/1750399X.2014.908558.

Incalcaterra McLoughlin, Laura – Jennifer Lertola
2015 "Captioning and Revoicing of Clips in Foreign Language Learning Using ClipFlair for Teaching Italian in Online Learning Environments", in Catherine Ramsey-Portolano (ed.), 55–69.

Jankowska, Agnieszka – Agnieszka Szarkowska (eds.)
2014 *Przekładaniec. Audiodeskrypcja, 28*/2014, Wydawnictwo Uniwersytetu Jagiellońskiego, Kraków.

Kilickaya, Ferit
2004 "Authentic materials and cultural content in EFL classroom", *The Internet TESL Journal X*(7), (Available at: http://iteslj.org/Techniques/Kilickaya-AutenticMaterial.html (date of access: 26 September 2015).

Komorowska, Hanna (ed.)
2011 *Issues in Promoting Multilingualism.* Warszawa: Fundacja Rozwoju Systemu Edukacji.

Lamie, M. Judit
2005 *Evaluating Change in English Language Teaching.* Houndmills, New York: Palgrave Macmillan.

Markham, Paul – Peter Lizette
2002 "The influence of English language and Spanish language captions on foreign language listening/reading comprehension," *Journal of Educational Technology Systems, 31*(3), 331–41.

O'Regan, John Kevin – Ariane Lévy-Schoen (eds.)
1987 *Eye Movements: From Psychology to Cognition.* Amsterdam: North-Holland.

Pérez-González, Luis
2009 "Audiovisual Translation", in Mona Baker - Gabriela Saldanha (eds.), 13–20.

Ramsey-Portolano, Catherine (ed.)
2015 *The Future of Italian Teaching; Media New Technologies and Multi-Disciplinary Perspectives*. Newcastle upon Tyne: Cambridge Scholars Publishing.

Sadowska, Anna
2014 Audiodeskrypcja do ilustracji w prasie – wskazówki dla trenerów szkolących audio deskryptorów, in Agnieszka Jankowska - Agnieszka Szarkowska (eds.), 124–139.

Sokoli, Stavroula – Patrick Zabalbescoa – Maria Fountana
2011 "Subtitling activities for foreign language learning: What learners and teachers think", in Laura Incalcaterra McLoughlin - Marie Biscio - Márie Á. Ní Mhainnín (eds.), 219–242.

Szymańska, Barbara – Tomasz Strzymiński
2010 *Standardy tworzenia audiodeskrypcji do produkcji audiowizualnych*. Białystok: Fundacja Audiodeskrypcja, Available at: http://avt.ils.uw.edu.pl/files/2010/12/AD-_standardy_tworzenia.pdf (date of access: 26 September 2015).

Talaván, Noa
2010 "Subtitling as a task and subtitles as support: Pedagogical applications", in Jorge Díaz Cintas - Anna Matamala - Joselia Neves (eds.), 285–299.

Tomaszkiewicz, Teresa
2009 "Linguistic and semiotic approaches to audiovisual translation", in Maria Freddi and Maria Pavesi (eds.), 19–29.

Van de Poel, Marijke – Géry d'Ydewalle
2001 "Incidental foreign-language acquisition by children watching subtitled television programs", in Yves Gambier and Henrik Gottlieb (eds.), 259–73.

Vanderplank, Robert
1990 "Paying attention to the words: Practical and theoretical problems in watching television programmes with uni-lingual (CEEFAX) subtitles", *System*, *18*, 221–34.

Walczak, Agnieszka
2013 *Films with Audio Description as an Additional Didactic Tool in Foreign Language Learning. A Case Study with School Children with and without Vision Impairments*. A presentation at Advanced Research Seminar in Audio Description in Barcelona, 13–14 March 2013.

Werner, Emilia
2010 „Świadomość innowacyjna społeczeństwa", in Lidia Białoń (ed.), 419–472.

Winterhoff-Spurk, Peter – Tom H.A. van der Voort (eds.)
1997 *New Horizons in Media Psychology*. Opladen: Westdeutcher Verlag.

Zabalbeascoa, Patrick - Stavroula Sokoli - Olga Torres (eds.)
2012 *CLIPFLAIR Foreign Language Learning Through Interactive Revoicing and Captioning of Clips. Lifelong Learning Programme – Key Activity 2. Language Multilateral Project. D2.1 Conceptual Framework and Pedagogical Methodology*. Available at: http://clipflair.net/wpcontent/uploads/2013/04/D2.1ConceptualFramework.pdf (date of access: 26 September 2015).

Ferit Kılıçkaya
Mehmet Akif Ersoy University, Burdur, Turkey

Use of Screencasting for Delivering Lectures and Providing Feedback in Educational Contexts: Issues and Implications

Abstract
There are a variety of factors that affect learning and teaching in educational contexts. Among these factors, teachers play an important role in student learning. Teachers not only deliver materials to learners but also guide learners in their learning experiences. While doing this, teachers allow learners to notice the progress they have been making and motivate them to further improve their skills. Teachers also benefit from the tools technology provides to them, such as screencasting. A screencast is a digital recording of the computer screen output, including audio narration, which was first implemented in order to show learners how to use computer software through demonstrations. Since then, it has also been used in educational contexts e.g. to deliver lectures and to provide feedback. This chapter aims to review the utilisation of screencasting in educational contexts and issues which can potentially emerge in the course of it. With this aim in mind, a brief discussion of screencasting is provided, followed by a review of studies within two streams of research which focus on the use of screencasting for delivering lectures and giving feedback. On the basis of the findings presented, several implications and suggestions have been proposed.

Keywords: screencasting, feedback, educational contexts

1. Introduction

Learning and teaching are affected by numerous factors, such as learning contexts, materials used, and teachers. Among these, motivation gains great importance. As Dörnyei et al. (2015: 72) state, "It [motivation] provides the primary impetus to initiate L2 learning and later the driving force to sustain the long, often tedious learning process; indeed, all the other factors involved in SLA presuppose motivation to some extent".

There are several issues that need attention while trying to increase students' motivation since a variety of factors can affect learning and teaching. As stated by Harmer (2007: 99), learning and teaching a foreign language may be influenced by "the society we live in" and by "the people around us". Teachers act as one of the most prominent motivational stimuli because they are involved in any stage of the learning process. Teachers' attitudes towards the target language and students play a crucial role in a teaching and learning setting as they are considered a precondition for success and an anxiety-free atmosphere in the classroom.

It is generally acknowledged that motivation is to be created, fostered, and maintained by enthusiastic and well-prepared teachers. Teachers have a variety of social functions that help students achieve learning outcomes. Lewis (2002: 30) states that teachers may have such roles as "baby-sitter", "student resource", "language advisor", "dictator", and "motivator". Certain roles, e.g. "motivator" and "language advisor", are highly valued in language classrooms, while others, such as "representative of author", are not.

Another important source of motivation for both underachievers and high achievers in the language classroom is the feedback provided (Henderson et al. 2014). Feedback on learners' progress seems to be a key factor in keeping learners motivated; as Williams et al. (1997:136) state,

> When feedback actually provides information to learners that enable them to identify specific aspects of their performance, it should prove both motivating and helpful to them to move into the zone of next development. If, on the other hand, the feedback fails to provide this kind of information, it could have entirely the opposite effect.

2. Ways of providing feedback

Providing feedback to language learners is crucial as it not only allows learners to notice the mistakes and progress they make but also motivates them to further improve their level of target language competence. Learners need feedback, including corrective feedback, particularly while they are dealing with writing and speaking activities in the target language. They need teachers' comments, suggestions and corrections to improve their proficiency in the target language. Teachers can provide feedback to learners in various forms. It may be provided to individual students, a group of students or the whole class. For written work, feedback may take the form of written comments and suggestions on paper, and while students are speaking, it might be oral. In either case, the main aim of providing feedback is to help learners, by any means possible, notice the language points to be improved and make them act upon the problematic areas accordingly.

With the emergence of technological tools, the ways of providing feedback have changed. Technological tools, such as word processing software, have paved the way for teachers to provide detailed responses to learners' written work (Walker et al. 2013). Furthermore, screencasting, which for years was mainly used to teach how to use computer software through demonstration, has recently changed the direction in giving feedback (Stannard 2008) and gained importance in educational contexts, especially in providing feedback to learners on their written work.

Traditionally, teachers provide feedback by making handwritten comments on students' work by highlighting the mistakes, underlining the unclear points, and making suggestions regarding both the content and the mechanics of writing. However, by using a screen recorder, teachers can record a video in which they comment and make suggestions on students' typed and/or handwritten work. The main advantage of this type of feedback is that the video including comments, corrections or suggestions can be played, paused or rewound by students as much as they like while they are revising their work based on the oral and visual feedback. It is also possible for teachers to provide more information to students about their work compared to the written commentary.

3. Screencasting

Screencasting is basically a digital recording of the computer screen output, often including audio narration. Screencasting is different from screen shooting or screen capturing in that the former contains video captures - visual components similar to a movie - of the computer screen activity accompanied by audio, while the latter provides images of the screen content at a particular time. There are a variety of tools available that can be used to create screencasts (Stannard 2008; Seery 2010; Hynson 2012; Kiliçkaya 2012; Stieglitz 2013; Siegle 2014; Luongo 2015). Some of them are commercial; however, others are freely available on the Internet, as presented in Table 1.

Table 1. Tools/websites to create screencasts

Tool/Website	URL	Basic Description
BB Flashback Express	http://www.bbsoftware.co.uk/BBFlashBack_FreePlayer.aspx	It allows recording the screen, with sound and webcam footage, in Flash and AVI formats. It is provided free of charge.
Camstudio	http://camstudio.org	It records screen and audio activity in AVI format. It is provided free of charge.
Camtasia Studio	https://www.techsmith.com/camtasia.html	It is a professional tool used to capture and record activities on the computer screen. Moreover, it is also equipped with a video editor. The price is around $300.

Tool/Website	URL	Basic Description
Freescreencast	www.freescreencast.com	It is free software with which to create quality screencasts. It also hosts the screencasts.
iSHOWYOU	http://shinywhitebox.com/ishowu	It is a screen recorder for Mac computers. The basic version can be purchased at $20.
Jing	https://www.techsmith.com/download/jing	It captures images and records video on the computer, adding visual elements. It is provided free of charge, but the output is limited to five minutes worth of recording.
Open Broadcaster	https://obsproject.com/	It is open source software for screen recording and live streaming, which is provided free of charge.
Screencast-o-matic	http://www.screencast-o-matic.com/	It captures the screen on Windows or Mac computers. It is possible to record online without downloading the software, or alternatively, with an installable application. The free version has recording time limitations.
ScreenFlow	http://www.telestream.net/screenflow/	It is screencasting and video editing software for Mac computers, which costs around $100.
Screenr	https://www.screenr.com/	It is a Web-based screen recorder that can be used without installation. The screencasts are hosted on the purveyor's website, and the recorder is provided free of charge.
Wink	http://www.debugmode.com/wink/	It is primarily aimed at creating tutorials and presentations. It allows saving a variety of outputs and is provided free of charge.

4. Studies on the use of screencasting in educational contexts

Several studies have been conducted on the use of screencasting in educational contexts, which fall into two streams: the studies which focus on the use of screencasting for delivering lectures and those that examine the utilisation of screencasting for providing feedback. Particular studies within the former stream of research focus on students' academic achievement (Oehrli et al. 2011; Mohamad Ali et al. 2011; Green et al. 2012; Lloyd et al. 2012; Tekinarslan 2013; Guerrero et al. 2013; Morris et al. 2014; Snyder et al. 2014), while others explore students' perceptions towards screencasting (Ford et al. 2012; Marriott et al. 2012; Sadik 2015). Within the latter stream, the studies investigate the effects of screencast feedback as well as students' perceptions of this form of feedback (Haxton et al. 2011; Edwards et al. 2012; Mathieson 2012; Séror, 2012; Thompson et al. 2012; Vincelette et al. 2013; Ahmat et al. 2013; Langton, 2015; Harper et al. 2015). Table 2 provides the aim of these studies as well as the tool used to create screencasts.

Table 2. List of studies on the use of screencasting in educational contexts

Authors	Year	Focus of the Study	Tool/Website	Use
Oehrli et al.	2011	To determine whether screencasts based on library resources facilitate student learning	ScreenFlow	Lectures
Haxton et al.	2011	To explore the perceptions of the students enrolled in a chemistry class where model answers and feedback were provided through screencasts	Camtasia Studio 7	Feedback
Mohamad Ali et al.	2011	To compare materials created using Camtasia Studio, with/without narration	Camtasia Studio	Lectures
Thompson et al.	2012	To explore students' perceptions of the use of screencasts provided as video feedback	Jing	Feedback
Green et al.	2012	To explore students' perceptions of the use of screencasts	no data	Lectures
Mathieson	2012	To explore students' perceptions of audio-visual feedback provided through screencasting as a supplement to traditional feedback (text-only)	Jing	Feedback
Ford et al.	2012	To explore students' perceptions of the use of recorded lectures and the effect of this on students' academic performance	Echo360 classroom capture system	Lectures

Authors	**Year**	**Focus of the Study**	**Tool/Website**	**Use**
Marriott et al.	2012	To explore students' perceptions and preferences regarding the feedback provided through screencasts	CamStudio	Feedback
Edwards et al.	2012	To explore the use of audio-visual screencasting to provide feedback on student assignments in a distance learning course	Jing	Feedback
Lloyd et al.	2012	To determine the effects of screencasts on learning outcomes in a psychology course in statistics	iShowU & iMovieMaker	Lectures
Séror	2012	To reflect on his own experiences on giving screencast feedback	Jing	Feedback
Guerrero et al.	2013	To investigate the effects of screencast lectures before and after the class in a mathematics for elementary teachers course at university level	no data	Lectures
Ahmad et al.	2013	To investigate the effects of instructor-developed screencasts on students' learning in a mathematics course at a higher education institution	no data	Lectures
Vincelette et al.	2013	To determine students' and instructors' perceptions of feedback provided via screencasting and to compare this form of feedback to traditional written or digital text-based comments and suggestions in a writing class	Jing	Feedback
Tekinarslan	2013	To determine the impact of screencasts on undergraduate students' achievement in a course in spreadsheet applications	Camtasia Studio	Lectures
Snyder et al.	2014	To study the effects of the screencasts developed by a social studies educator on students' engagement in three ninth-grade world history classes	ScreenFlow	Lectures

Authors	Year	Focus of the Study	Tool/Website	Use
Morris et al.	2014	To investigate the impact of screencasts on knowledge acquisition	PowerPoint slides synchronized with audio	Lectures
Langton	2015	To determine the benefits and drawbacks of providing feedback through screencasts in a Japanese class	Mediasite	Feedback
Harper	2015	To analyze the effects of screencasts created for individual feedback on foreign language students' written assignments	Jing	Feedback
Sadik	2015	To determine students' preferences regarding lecture captures and screencast recordings as supplements to classroom lectures	HD Video and Presentation Tube	Feedback

4.1. Screencast lectures and student academic achievement

Oehrli et al. (2011) investigated whether students as inexperienced library users could learn from screencasts basing on library resources. The study included a pre- and post-test including a series of three tasks, such as clicking on the image, where the participants would begin search for an appropriate library database to find resources for an assignment. The study suggested that screencasts facilitate student learning as most students learnt how to complete a multi-step research process by using instructional screencasts.

In another study, Mohamad Ali et al. (2011) used screencast software *Camtasia Studio* to teach Flash animation software functions, such as timeline and drawing tools. The participants in one group studied a screencast series without narration, while those in the other group watched the screencast series with narration. The results of the study indicated that short instructional materials with narration promote learning better, especially for students with little prior knowledge on the course content. The results also indicated that instructional materials prepared by using screencasting software can support online self-paced learning.

Green et al. (2012) explored through a survey engineering students' perceptions of the usefulness of screencasts. The study focused on how and why students used, or did not choose to use, screencasts. The findings of the study indicated that the participants using screencasts seemed to have increased their understanding of the content, as indicated by the exam results. Lloyd et al. (2012), on the other hand, aimed to determine the effects of screencast tutorials on learning outcomes in statistics. The study included students from four sections of a statistics course offered in the Department of Psychology at a public university. The students were randomly assigned to two groups, where one group followed the traditional approach, while the other was exposed to video tutorials created as screencasts by using iShowU and iMovieMaker. The task required the students to solve a novel statistical problem. The results of the study indicated that the video tutorials based on screencasts proved to be an efficient and effective tool as they enhanced learning. Screencasts were found to be particularly useful for higher order conceptual statistical knowledge.

A recent study conducted by Tekinarslan (2013) investigated the impact of screencasts on undergraduate students' achievement in spreadsheet applications. The study used experimental design, where the participants in the experimental group benefited from screencasts published in a social networking environment, while those in the control group were not provided with digital records of screen activities in the spreadsheet applications in question. Both groups were given the same multiple-choice and practical post-tests. The results showed that the students from the experimental group scored higher on the multiple-choice and practical post-tests than their counterparts from the control group.

Guerrero et al. (2013) investigated the effects of screencast lectures before and after the class in a university level course entitled Mathematics for Elementary Teachers. The participants were students enrolled in that course, and they were divided into two groups. In one group the students were exposed to screencast lectures, while in the other they received traditional non-digital instruction. The data collection instruments included a pre-post context exam, an attitude survey as well as student responses to an open-ended prompt regarding the use of video lectures. The students who received screencast lectures were found to be more successful considering the examination scores which they obtained compared to the others who had not been exposed to digital lectures. Moreover, the findings revealed that screencast lectures saved class time for student-centered and problem-solving activities, leading to positive student attitudes.

In a more recent study, Morris et al. (2014) analyzed the effect of screencasts on undergraduate students' knowledge acquisition. The screencasts were used as a supplement to classroom lectures, rather than a substitute for them and featured a set of PowerPoint slides that were synchronized with the audio recordings of the lecturer. Additionally, they included subtitles whenever important points required highlighting. The students from the experimental group were encouraged to access the screencasts through the Blackboard website, while the students from the control group did not access the screencasts at all. The examination consisting of multiple-choice questions on the lectures and practical handbooks revealed that the screencasts had a significant impact on knowledge acquisition in favor of the experimental group. The results also suggested that the students in the experimental group highly valued the use of screencasts.

In an action research study, Snyder et al. (2014) explored the effects of screencasts developed by a social studies educator on students' engagement in three ninth-grade world history classes offered in a public school. The screencasts included PowerPoint slides with images and documents. The educator talked to the students through a thumbnail-sized video in the PowerPoint slides. The results of the study revealed that the students watching the screencasts were more engaged in the activities in the classroom. The students also mentioned several benefits of the screencasts, e.g. the ability to pause the videos to take notes at their own pace. Moreover, the results also indicated that the educator could devote more time to student-centered and inquiry-based learning activities in the classroom.

The studies briefly overviewed in this section clearly indicate that lectures and/or tutorials delivered through screencasts facilitate learning. Short instructional materials with narration have been found to better promote learning, especially for learners with low prior knowledge of the course content. Moreover, ensuing self-paced learning is highly valued by learners as screencasts enable them to watch and listen to the lectures as many times as they wish at their own pace. Another common benefit of screencasts is that learners retain more knowledge through screencasts. When screencasts supplement in-class activities, it has been observed that classroom time can be saved for student-centered and inquiry-based learning activities.

4.2. Screencast lectures and student perceptions

Ford et al. (2012) investigated the benefits of screencasting technology as a supplementary resource in a traditional lecture-based class. The study implemented the Echo360 classroom capture system in order to record lectures delivered by an instructor with the use of a whiteboard and PowerPoint presentations. Out of the four student groups under investigation, two were allowed to access the recorded lectures through a course management system, while the other two were not exposed to the recordings. The results suggested that recorded lectures led to positive student perceptions. However, these positive perceptions were not reflected in the course grades. In other words, no association was detected between the use of recorded lectures and the level of student achievement.

Marriott et al. (2012) aimed to explore students' perceptions and preferences regarding feedback provided via screencasts. The participants of the study were students enrolled in a compulsory 15-credit Managing Finance module, covering the fundamental concepts of management accounting for business. As a requirement of the module, the students worked in pairs, prepared coursework and shared it electronically with their tutor by uploading it to the university network. The coursework submitted was then evaluated by the tutor, who recorded feedback in the form of video footage by using CamStudio, the free screen recording software. The students who received the feedback through screencasts were then invited to participate in an online quiz. Moreover, focus group meetings were held with selected students. The results of the study revealed that the majority of the students had positive attitudes towards feedback provided through screencasts and they enumerated several benefits of this form of feedback e.g. its more personal/individualised character and the ability to follow a combination of audio comments.

A very recent study conducted by Sadik (2015) investigated students' preferences regarding the use of lecture captures and screencasts as supplements to classroom lectures. The participants of the study included undergraduate students registered in two courses: distance education and evaluation in educational technology. The classrooms where students studied traditionally were recorded by the lecturers using a single HD video camera, while the PresentationTube screencasting software was used to simulate classroom lectures. These two types of recordings were shared with the students and their views were analyzed. The findings revealed that both types of recordings proved to be useful as supplements to student learning; however, the majority of the students considered screencasts better than lecture captures for a number of reasons, including the quality of the audio.

The common finding of the studies reviewed in this section is that the majority of the students exposed to screencast lectures had positive attitudes towards the solution and valued screencasts highly.

4.3. Screencast feedback

Haxton et al. (2011) studied the perceptions of students enrolled in a chemistry class where model answers and feedback were provided through screencasts created with the use of Camtasia Studio. The level of feedback was limited to only the key points and uncommon errors made by the students. The key finding of the study was that the production of screencast feedback was found to be time-consuming by the tutors. However, the students found the experience invaluable as they felt that the screencast feedback was equal to, or better than, written feedback in terms of quality and quantity.

In another study, conducted by Thompson et al. in 2012, screencasts were prepared using the Jing software in order to share the instructors' feedback on the students' written essays. The students were surveyed about the feedback provided through videos which included the instructors' comments and suggestions. As the results of the study revealed, the participants were positive about the use of digital feedback and they highly valued the comments delivered electronically. The results also indicated that video feedback was found to be effective, especially during the revision process, as the students tried to make global changes to their essays, rather than simply apply changes to specific lexical or grammatical items.

Edwards et al. (2012) explored the use of audio-visual screencasting to provide feedback on student assignments in a distance learning course. The participants of the study were students enrolled on a communication ethics module. The screencast feedback was provided on student assignments using Jing. The results of the study suggested that screencast feedback provided was viewed more positively compared to the written feedback, as the visual cues and explanations included in the screencasts reportedly increased the students' understanding of the information provided.

Mathieson (2012), on the other hand, explored students' perceptions of audio-visual feedback through screencasting as a supplement to traditional, text-only feedback. The study was conducted on undergraduate students enrolled on a statistics course and a research methodology course. All the students were exposed to both text-only and text-plus-audio visual feedback and the students' perceptions were analysed through an open-ended survey. The results showed that the students considered text-plus-audio-visual feedback effective as it allowed them to interact with the instructor in a more real and personal way. For example, as one of the participants stated, "For me the more effective way of interacting with the instructor was the text-plus-audiovisual because it gave me a classroom-like feel listening to my instructor with both my visual and hearing senses working at the same time" (Mathieson, 2012: 150).

Séror (2012), based on his own experiences with students in his classes, stated that the students' responses were positive towards screencasting as a feedback tool. Although some of his students found screencasts long to listen to, they valued this form of audio-visual feedback. A similar study, conducted by Vincelette et al. (2013), aimed to determine both students' and instructors' perceptions of feedback provided by using screencasting and to compare this form of feedback to traditional written or digital text-based comments and suggestions. The study involved 39 college students enrolled on one of the two entry-level compulsory composition classes. The course instructors created five-minute screencasts using Jing in order to deliver their comments and suggestions on the students' written work. The results of the study revealed that the students perceived screencast feedback on their written papers as more effective than traditional feedback provided through written comments and suggestions. It occurred that the students attended to revisions delivered electronically more effectively. The instructors also felt that screencasts changed the way they provided feedback in terms of length and the level of detail, while the students' responses to the comments and suggestions were also more positive. As one of the instructors involved in the study stated, "They [students] liked the personal attention, they felt they understood the feedback more than just the written comments, and they felt a little more personable towards me." (Vincelette et al. 2013: 266) However, the instructors were found to worry about technical issues, such as using and editing the program to create screencasts as well as the time spent on creating screencasts.

Ahmad et al. (2013), in a case study which they conducted, investigated the effects of instructor-developed screencasts on students' learning of mathematics in a higher education institution. 47 screencasts were developed by the instructor and uploaded to a Moodle site for students' access. The participants of the study provided their views on the screencasts through an online open-ended survey, and their responses were analysed by using thematic content analysis. The analysis of the responses indicated that the majority of the students used these screencasts for a variety of purposes, such as material review, exam revision, and learning key maths concepts. As it turned out, the students valued the multimodal support provided by the screencasts. The findings also supported the idea that screencasts can be used to facilitate and enhance students' learning.

Langton (2015) conducted a case study in order to determine the benefits and drawbacks of providing feedback through screencasts. The study focused on two students of different levels of proficiency in English. They were asked to submit their drafts and revised essays on two different topics over the course of a term. Conventional written feedback was provided on one assignment, while screencast feedback was utilized on the other. The feedback in both forms focused on grammatical accuracy, style, and organization. The responses obtained indicated that one student believed that screencast feedback provided more detailed explanations and examples compared to conventional feedback, while the other student favoured conventional written feedback as it was easier for them to see the written feedback, rather than watch it.

In a recent study Harper et al. (2015) investigated whether screencasts created for individual feedback on foreign language students' written assignments would make any difference to the tutors' and students' experience. The study also focused on how error correction and written feedback could be enhanced through the use of personalized screencasts. The screencasts containing feedback on the students' written assignments were created using the screencasting software Jing and were shared with the students. The findings of the study revealed promising benefits of screencasting. The students as well as the tutors found that the format facilitated student-tutor communication. The students particularly valued the opportunity to listen to the tutor while s/he was explaining the corrections, suggestions, and comments on the written work. The feedback provided via screencasting software was also found to be more detailed compared to the traditional written feedback.

The participants of the studies discussed in this section highly valued screencast feedback, stating several benefits of this form of feedback, such as more personal comments on their written work provided through both visual and auditory channels. However, the key issue raised by the instructors is that delivering screencast feedback requires a large amount of time.

5. Pedagogical implications

Based on the results of the studies reviewed and the literature on the use of screencasting for delivering lectures and providing feedback, the following suggestions can be listed:

- Mainly used for teaching how to perform operations on computers through demonstrations, screencasts also have the potential to serve as a means through which to deliver lectures, especially online lectures both before and after face-to-face classes, and to provide feedback on students' written work. Screencasts allow flexibility in the speed at which learners may want to progress through the content. Some learners may need to review content several times in order to learn it effectively. Therefore, screencasts play an important role in self-paced learning.
- As research indicates, screencast lectures should not be long, from five to 10 minutes, and should focus on major issues in the course content rather than minor ones. However, some students might prefer audio format to screencast lectures created with PowerPoint slides (Garner, 2008) as audio files can be played by a variety of devices, leading to flexibility in terms of use. Students might like to print the PowerPoint slides and play the audio files on their portable music players and review the notes at any time and in any place.

The solution, then, would be to provide both video and audio versions of the screencasts.

- Oral and visual feedback provided through screencasts, which is not available in written comments on students' works, enables learners to easily follow instructions, with the opportunity to revise comments and suggestions as many times as they need to. Screencasts may clarify the meaning and focus on more individualized feedback, thus, they permit students to have a strong connection with their teachers. This proves to be particularly useful for distance education programmes, where face-to-face meetings and individual writing conferences are not feasible. Educators teaching in face-to-face classrooms may also try to use screencasts as this form of feedback has been found to provide greater detail.
- Another important issue that should be considered is the habit of working on paper. Both teachers and students should be aware that getting used to different modes of delivery may take time as it may not be easy for teachers to get out of the habit of reading written work and providing written comments. Similarly, students may find it hard to get out of the habit of listening to lectures in the classroom and interacting with the lecturer.
- The main issue and challenge in creating screencasts for both delivering lectures and providing feedback is the time required to do so, which will depend on the lecture content and the type of written work being marked as well as the comprehensibility of feedback. Learning how to create screencasts might be very demanding and time-consuming for those who will use screencasting for the first time. Since the research shows that creating screencast feedback and sending recorded videos to learners may take more time than providing written feedback, it might be suggested that screencast feedback is not feasible for large classes.
- Another issue is related to the re-use of screencasts. The nature of lecture screencasts allows teachers to re-use them in future classes whenever they find it appropriate; however, it is not the same case with the screencast feedback, which is geared towards individual learners.
- Last but not least, selecting a screencast tool requires careful consideration (see Table 1 for a list of screencasting websites and tools). A benefit-cost analysis should be conducted before making the choice. While some of the tools are freely available, they may have certain limitations, and they may fail to provide more advanced features, such as output editing.

References

Ahmad, Tunku – Badariah Tunku – Frank Doheny – Sheil Faherty – Nuala Harding
2013 "How instructor-developed screencasts benefit college students' learning of Maths: Insights from an Irish case study", *The Malaysian Online Journal of Educational Technology 1*(4), 12–25. Available at: http://www.mojet.net/frontend/articles/pdf/v01i04/v01i04-02.pdf (date of access: August 30, 2015).

Dörnyei, Zoltán – Stephen Ryan
2015 *The Psychology of the Language Learner Revisited.* New York, NY: Routledge.

Edwards, Kirstie – Anne-Florence Dujardin – Noel Williams
2012 "Screencast feedback for essays on a distance learning MA in professional communication: An action research project", *Journal of Academic Writing, 2*(1): 95–126. Available at: http://e-learning.coventry.ac.uk/ojs/index.php/joaw/article/view/62/105 (date of access: August 14 2015).

Ford, Máire B. – Colleen E. Burns – Nathan Mitch – Melissa M. Gomez.
2012 "The effectiveness of classroom capture technology", *Active Learning in Higher Education, 13*(3), 191–201.

Garner, Stuart
2008 "The use of screencasting and audio to support student learning", in Joseph Luca - Edgar R. Weippl (eds.), *Proceedings of EdMedia: World Conference on Educational Media and Technology, 2008*, 4693–4698. Association for the Advancement of Computing in Education (AACE).

Green, Katie R. – Tershia Pinder-Grover – Joanna Millunchick Mirecki
2012 "Impact of screencast technology: Connecting the perception of usefulness and the reality of performance", *Journal of Engineering Education, 101*(4), 717–737.

Guerrero, Shannon – Drew Baumgartel – Maren Zobott
2013 "The use of screencasting to transform traditional pedagogy in a preservice Mathematics content course", *Journal of Computers in Mathematics and Science Teaching, 32*(2), 173–193.

Harmer, Jeremy
2007 *The Practice of English Language Teaching* (4th ed.) Harlow: Pearson Education.

Harper, Felicity – Hannelore Green – Maria Fernandez-Toro
2015 "Using screencasts in the teaching of modern languages: investigating the use of Jing® in feedback on written assignments", *The Language Learning Journal.* http://dx.doi.org/10.1080/09571736.2015.1061586

Haxton, Katherine J. – David J. McGarvey
2011 "Screencasting as a means of providing timely, general feedback on assessment", *New Directions, 7*, 18–21. Available at: https://www.heacademy.ac.uk/sites/default/files/ndir.1.7f.pdf (date of access: August 10, 2015).

Henderson, Michael – Michael Phillips
2014 "Technology enhanced feedback on assessment". Paper presented at *the Australian Computers in Education Conference 2014*, Adelaide, SA. Available at: http://acec2014.acce.edu.au/session/technology-enhanced-feedback-assessment (date of access: 13 September 2015).

Hynson, Yvonne T. A.
2012 "An innovative alternative to providing writing feedback on students' essays", *Teaching English with Technology, 12*(1), 53–57. Available at: http://tewtjournal.org/issues/past-issue-2012/past-issue-2012-issue-1/ (Date of access: 12 September 2015).

Kılıçkaya, Ferit
2012 "Providing feedback to language learners through screencasting software", *The AATSEEL Newsletter, 55*(3), 7–12. Available at: http://www.aatseel.org/100111/pdf/aatseeloct12nl.pdf (date of access: 15 August 2015).

Langton, Nina
2015 "Elaborated feedback for beginning Japanese language students: The benefits and drawbacks of screencast delivery", *CAJLE Proceedings 2015*, 142–149. Available at: http://www.jp.cajle.info/wp-content/uploads/2015/09/16_Langton_CAJLE2015Proceedings_142-149.pdf (date of access: September 25 2015).

Lewis, Michael
2002 *The Lexical Approach: The State of ELT and a Way Forward*. Boston, MA: Heinle.

Lloyd, Steven A. – Chuck L. Robertson
2012 "Screencast tutorials enhance student learning of Statistics", *Teaching of Psychology, 39*(1), 67–71.

Luongo, Nicole
2015 "Missing the chalkboard: Using screencasting in the online classroom", *Computers in the Schools: Interdisciplinary Journal of Practice, Theory, and Applied Research, 32*(2), 144–151.

Marriott, Pru – Lim Keong Teoh
2012 "Using screencasts to enhance assessment feedback: Students' perceptions and preferences", *Accounting Education: An International Journal, 21*(6), 583–598.

Mathieson, Kathleen
2012 "Exploring student perceptions of audiovisual feedback via screencasting in online courses", *American Journal of Distance Education, 26*(3), 143–156.

Mohamad Ali – Ahmad Zamzuri – Khairulanuar Samsudin – Mohamad Hassan – Salman Firdaus Sidek
2011 "Does screencast teaching software application needs narration for effective learning?", *Turkish Online Journal of Educational Technology 10*(3), 76–82. Available at http://www.tojet.net/articles/v10i3/1039.pdf (date of access: September 20, 2015).

Morris, Cecile – Gladson Chikwa
2014 "Screencasts: How effective are they and how do students engage with them?", *Active Learning in Higher Education, 15*(1), 25–37.

Oehrli, Jo Angela – Julie Piacentine – Amanda Peters – Benjamin Nanamaker
2011 "Do screencasts really work? Assessing student learning through instructional screencasts." *ACRL Annual Conference*, 127–144. Philadelphia, Pennsylvania. Available at: http://www.ala.org/acrl/sites/ala.org.acrl/files/content/conferences/confsandpreconfs/national/2011/papers/do_screencasts_work.pdf (date of access: 14 August 2015).

Sadik, Alaa
2015 "Students' preferences for types of video lectures: Lecture capture vs. screencast recordings", *International Journal of Higher Education, 4*(4), 94–104. Available at: http://www.sciedu.ca/journal/index.php/ijhe/article/viewFile/7919/4719 (date of access: September 20 2015).

Seery, Michael K.
2010 "Podcasting and screencasting for supporting lecturers". Available at: http://www.dit.ie/lttc/media/ditlttc/documents/lttcresources/Screencasting%20and%20podcasting%20for%20supporting%20lectures.pdf (date of access: June 15, 2015).

Séror, Jérémie
2012 "Show me! Enhanced feedback through screencasting technology", *TESL Canada Journal, 30*(1), 104–116. Available at: http://www.teslcanadajournal.ca/index.php/tesl/article/viewFile/1128/947 (date of access: 20 September 2015).

Siegle, Del
2014 "Differentiating instruction by flipping the classroom", Gifted *Child Today, 37*(1), 51–55.

Snyder, Catherine – Lawrence M. Paska – David Besozzi
2014 "Cast from the past: Using screencasting in the social studies classroom", *The Social Studies, 105*(6), 310–314.

Stannard, Russell
2008 "A new direction in feedback", *Humanising Language Teaching, 6.* Available at: http://www.hltmag.co.uk/dec08/mart04.htm (date of access: September 10, 2015).

Stieglitz, Guy
2013 "Screencasting: Informing students, shaping instruction", *UAE Journal of Educational Technology and Elearning, 4,* 58–62. Available at: http://ejournal.hct.ac.ae/wp-content/uploads/2013_Article08.pdf (date of access: June 13, 2015).

Tekinarslan, Erkan
2013 "Effects of screencasting on the Turkish undergraduate students' achievement and knowledge acquisitions in spreadsheet applications", *Journal of Information Technology Education: Research, 12,* 271–282. Available at: http://www.jite.org/documents/Vol12/JITEv12ResearchP271-282Tekinarslan1250.pdf (date of access: 14 September 2015).

Thompson, Riki – Meredith J. Lee
2012 "Talking with students through screencasting: Experiments with video feedback to improve student learning", *The Journal of Interactive Technology and Pedagogy, 1.* Available at: http://jitp.commons.gc.cuny.edu/2012/table-of-contents-issue-one/

Vincelette, Elizabeth Jackson – Timothy Bostic
2013 "Show and tell: Student and instructor perceptions of screencast assessment", *Assessing Writing, 18,* 257–277.

Walker, Aisha – Goodith White
2013 *Technology Enhanced Language Learning: Connecting Theory and Practice.* Oxford, UK: Cambridge University Press.

Williams, Marion – Robert L. Burden
1997 *Psychology for Language Teachers: A Social Constructivist Approach.* Cambridge: Cambridge University Press.

Przemysław Krakowian
University of Łódź, Łódź, Poland

Promoting Self-reflection in Assessment of Intercultural Communicative Competence in Professional Contexts via the Web

Abstract
All across the globe, with but a few notable exceptions, we live in speaking-dominated cultures, where expression is considered paramount to communication. So, what makes a good speaker and communicator? What is communicative language ability? What is communicative competence in another language and how does culture motivate communication? Developing language skills for international communication is increasingly perceived as insufficient when viewed in traditional terms of communicative competence. Communication in international, multi-cultural professional settings, or as it is now referred to, intercultural professional communication, does not merely rely on language skills, but to a large extent on the ability to recognise, appreciate and deal with differences in which members of different cultures communicate. With this idea in mind, a European project CEF-cult, amongst other deliverables, developed a sustainable online platform geared towards honing the competences involved by providing authentic scenarios, validated assessment frameworks and a community of like-minded people with a view to promoting awareness and self-reflection when dealing with communication involving members of other cultures. The present chapter looks at how this Web-based platform encourages reflection and awareness of the differences between people in order to provide them with tools to resolve issues in communication. The online Web-based system described in the text below constitutes an interesting example of open educational resources (OER), not only because such resources rarely provide access to spoken learner language, but also because its focus is on the intercultural and cross-cultural aspects of international communication, which naturally results in opening language classrooms through intercultural exchanges. The author of this chapter was involved at the inception stage of the project aimed at the development of the system, contributed to the concept of the scenarios and the validation systems, and authored and co-authored several of the scenarios and assessment instances embedded in the resource.

Keywords: intercultural competence, assessment, CEFR, INCA scales, developing language skills, professional intercultural communication

1. Introduction

Initiated in November 2009 and completed in October 2011, the CEFcult project[1] aimed at enabling collaborative assessment of oral language proficiency and intercultural competence with the use of the INCA[2] scales through a Web 2.0 environment in professional settings. The underlying idea behind the project was that one major objective of language programmes deployed for professional purposes is to give the learners the opportunity and tools to see their foreign language experience in the context of not merely effective business and professional communication, but to do so in intercultural settings, something that in the globalized world is becoming a staple.

The significance of the intercultural element in both teaching and evaluation contexts has for a long time been appreciated in the EU programmes to promote language learning. The Council of Europe (2001, 2008) in their documents recognise that as a result of language learner exposure to numerous languages and cultures in the course of their education, they become multi- and pluri-lingual and develop sensitivity of the realities of other cultures, which is seen as becoming multi- and inter-cultural. Learner's communicative competences in other languages, as well as their competence in their native language, as a result become modified by the aspects of cultural knowledge they have been exposed to and the awareness they have gained. This, in turn, affects the ways in which they carry out their life routines, and amongst those, how they function professionally, both in mono- and multi-cultural settings.

While the layer of intercultural awareness adding to one's communicative competence, or to go one step further, one's intercultural communication competence (Byram 1997), is of substantial interest in many contexts and to many parties, with international professional communication being just one, this is an extremely difficult area to assess. It would, therefore, be useful to develop tools to measure both communicative language ability and intercultural awareness and competences. Assessing intercultural communication competence in terms of traditional assessment arrangements fails, as those are most commonly deployed within relatively rigid frameworks with closed scripts to ensure consistency of rating. Assessing intercultural aspects of communication in separation from, or on top of, communicative language ability is futile as cultural differences motivate the course of communication, and it is successful communication that determines how interculturally communicatively competent anyone is.

1 CEFcult http://cefcult.eu
2 INCA Project http://www.incaproject.org (as of late, support discontinued)

This chapter looks at the issue of assessing oral communication in professional settings with particular emphasis on those aspects of communication that can be potentially contributing factors in communication breakdown, misunderstandings and difficulties owing to cultural differences, differences in understanding other cultures in international settings and the role played by ethnocentrism in communicating with others. It looks at one available tool designed for this purpose in the form of a customisable, scenario-driven assessment Web-based platform.

2. Building scenarios and tasks in fostering intercultural awareness

The CEFcult platform, also referred to as the CEFcult Tool (http://cefcult.eu/tool), is a Web application whose functions fall into four categories: i) user management facility; ii) scenario builder; iii) assessment facility; iv) repository, of which the last three will be of interest here.

Figure 1. CEFcult tool start screen: scenario builder, assessment tool and scenario repository

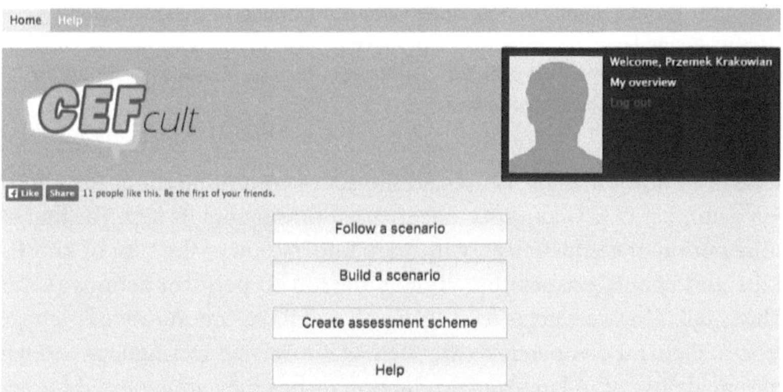

Scenarios can span from as simple as one screen to a range of subtasks, with each followed by subsequent tasks and responses. Scenarios are highly customisable, with the imagination of the creator and feasibility and doability of the scenario being the only limiting factors. Existing scenarios created by other users are also available to try and can be customised to suit particular needs by cutting down some of their features or by adding content appropriate for a particular situation or purpose. For a scenario to be complete, it needs to be fitted with assessment scales with the option to choose all or only selected suitable scales from a range of available frameworks. Additionally, the scenario builder allows the user to customise the assessment scales, or to render them in another language. Of the numerous frameworks for assessing intercultural competences available to date, the tool implements the Intercultural Competence Assessment (INCA) framework, based on work by Byram (1997) and others, which at the stage of deploying the tool was deemed by the project partners to be well in line with the Common European Framework of Reference for Languages (CEFR).

3. Rationale behind CEFR and INCA assessment scales

The Council of Europe (2001) through the CEFR looks at the communicative language use from two distinct perspectives. On the one hand, it postulates a range of general competences; and, on the other, it recognizes the existence of particular language competences. Both are necessary for successful communication and both refer to elements of one's own culture as well as features of other cultures.

> Language use [...] comprises the actions performed by persons who as individuals and as social agents develop a range of **competences**, both **general** and in particular **communicative language competences**. They draw on the competences at their disposal in various **contexts** under various conditions and under various constraints to engage in **language activities** involving language processes to produce and/or receive texts in relation to themes in specific **domains**, activating those strategies which seem most appropriate for carrying out the **tasks** to be accomplished.
>
> (COE 2001: 9; emphasis mine)

In explication of how language is used in the act of communication, the CEFR calls upon a number of key concepts that are used throughout its text. The first of those is the notion of competences, which are understood as the sum of knowledge, skills and characteristics that allow a person to perform actions (COE 2001). Those fall into two categories: i) general; and ii) communicative language competences. General competences are seen as not related to language though sometimes made use of in language production just as they are required for actions of all other kinds. General competences embrace various notions of culture, by which the CEFR understands one's own as well as other cultures the user has come in contact with. Communicative language competences, on the other hand, are those competences which are required explicitly for language use in acts of communication.

Context and conditions denote the arrangement of entities, concepts, events and setting factors, both tangible, physical and any other, internal, and personal as well as external, objectively observable, to which acts of communication are related and in relation to which they take place. When engaged in language activities, the participants' communicative language competences are implemented in relation to a domain in processing. This is understood as either receptive or productive, or consists of a combination of both, and may be sequential in some fashion, which happens when one or more texts are involved in carrying out a task. The notion of text refers to any portion of discourse, either spoken or written, which is inextricably related to a domain or theme understood as a sector of social life in which social agents operate, further broken down into the educational, occupational, public and personal domains (COE 2001), a lot of which are embedded in culture, and sometimes involving agents from different cultures negotiating tasks.

A task is perceived as any action aimed at achieving tangible influence on the outside world and producing a desired result in the context of a problem to be solved, an obligation to fulfil or an objective to be achieved, where a strategy consists of organised, purposeful and regulated sequence of actions the person elects to follow in order to achieve the task (COE 2001). All of the above requires and presupposes the involvement of language processes, which consist of the neurological and physiological phenomena comprising the production and processing of written and spoken discourse.

General competences are understood in the CEFR as a number of distinct competences and are further defined as:

- general knowledge, which is understood as declarative knowledge and is also referred to as *savoir*, is conceived of as any knowledge coming from experience, constituting empirical knowledge, but also as resulting from any type of formal learning comprising academic knowledge, with the presupposition that successful communication relies on the knowledge of the world which is shared by the participants of the acts of communication. The knowledge of the world additionally comprises the sociocultural knowledge, denoted as features uniquely characteristic of a particular target language society with respect to the awareness of everyday living, socio-geographically distinct living conditions, the scope of interpersonal relations, pervading values, beliefs and attitudes, acceptable body language, dominant social conventions and ritual behaviours;
- skills and know-how, or *savoir-faire*, is understood as the ability to create, act and perform activities aimed at manipulating, influencing and otherwise exerting power over the physical and non-physical arrangements in the surrounding world. Those are further sub-branched as individual skills and abilities with reference to various areas of human activity such as: social skills, which involve the capacity for proceeding in agreement with social conven-

tions characteristic of the type of setting involved; living skills, which embrace the potential to perform successfully everyday, habitual activities required in day-to-day operations and life; vocational and professional skills, involving the potential to execute specific physical and mental actions demanded in vocation and profession; leisure skills as in the ability to engage in and pursue leisure activities, pastimes and hobbies; most importantly from the perspective of a cross-cultural user, intercultural skills and know-how denoting the facility for integrating the native culture and the target culture; and, finally, cultural sensitivity, all of which is perceived as the command over a range of strategies for interacting with individuals from other cultures;

- existential competence, or *savoir-être*, which is seen as personal awareness and awareness of self or selfhood, made up of personality characteristics and traits, attitudes, drives, motivations, values, beliefs, cognitive styles, in short, what is believed by the CEFR authors to be personal identity;
- ability to learn alternatively, labelled as *savoir-apprendre*, which is responsible for an individual's capacity for observation and participation in novel experiences and for incorporating thus gained knowledge and experiences into existing knowledge. This is also seen as embracing strategies for knowledge acquisition as well as heuristic and cognitive skills, and skills necessary for understanding ideospheres and common collective consciousness different from ours, including the ability to reflect on the experience at hand.

The work of Byram (1997) and subsequently of other members of the INCA team resulted in the creation of a set of scales aimed at capturing the essence of those aspects of communication that can be seen as contributing to communication breakdown, misunderstandings and difficulties owing to cultural differences, differences in understanding other cultures and the role cultural identity plays in communication. As can be seen in Figure 2 below, a large portion of Byram's framework overlaps with what was captured in the rationale for the CEFR outlined above. Byram's 1997 and subsequently 2002 framework (Byram 1997, Byram et al. 2002) identifies three main components of intercultural competence: openness, adaptability and knowledge, each involving two further sub-components: respect for otherness and tolerance of ambiguity, behavioural flexibility and communicative awareness, and knowledge discovery and empathy, respectively. In terms of scales, it postulates descriptors for each of them, each time involving three bands relating to the level of proficiency, competence and experience.

Figure 2. Byram's Framework for Intercultural Communicative / Communication Competence (based on Byram 1997, Byram et al. 2002)

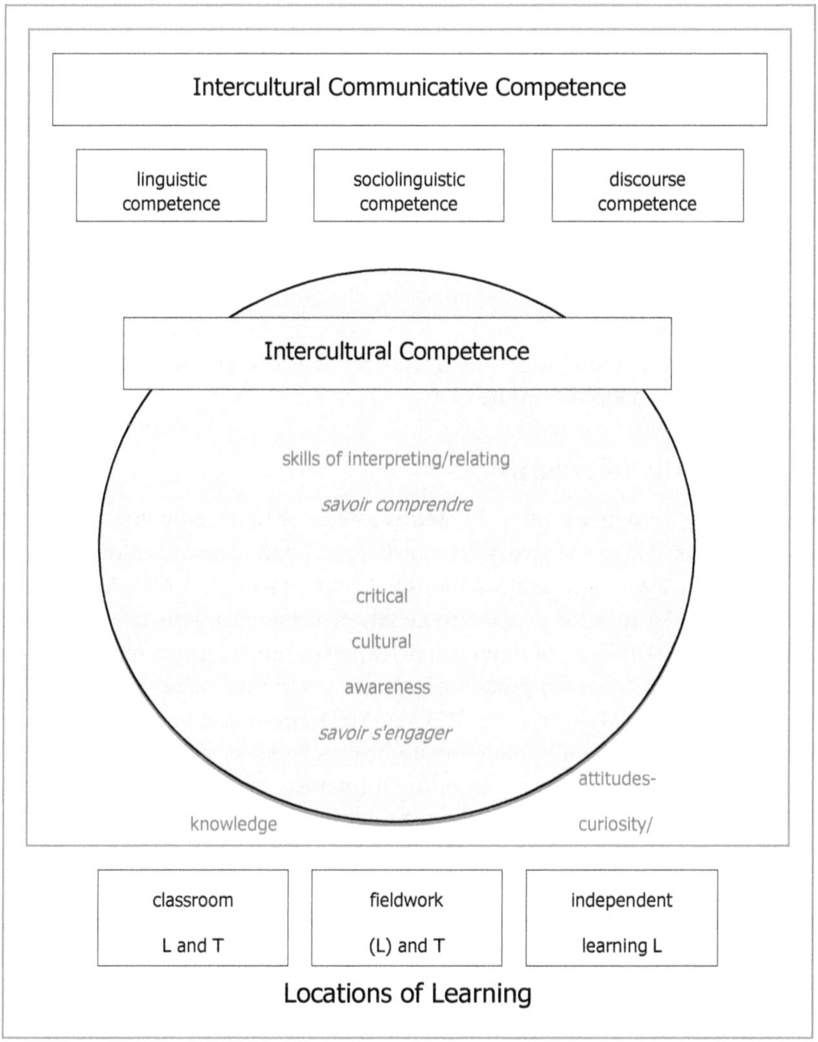

The framework is not only very much in line with how the CEFR understands communication and the underpinning skills and competences, but through its scales it additionally solely focuses on those aspects of communication that do not make it into assessment scales in the CEFR, and which are of paramount importance when communication takes place in multicultural settings, such as those on the international workplace.

4. Assessing communication using scenarios

With the scenario in place, a potential user, oftentimes not the creator himself, can select and work through various stages and tasks of it, providing responses in the form envisaged by the task author and creator, by either typing or selecting responses or using a webcam and microphone to record answers. The responses to the prompts in the scenario are then stored and made available upon request to the assessors to inspect. The responses can also be inspected by the participant allowing self-evaluation, and hopefully reflection, especially when one's own responses are compared with those of other assessors forming a Community of Practice (CoP), as the tool stores both responses as well as any instances of evaluation made by the members of the CoP.

5. Community of practice

A community of practice is often defined as a network or a forum, both informal and with varying degrees of formal structuring and internal organisation, through which ideas are exchanged and solutions generated (Wenger 1998). It often is a community of like-minded people, frequently professionals, associated with one another through similarity of interests and expertise, and working on a common set of problems, in common pursuit of solutions, and themselves constituting a store of knowledge (Wenger 1998; Wenger, McDermott and Snyder 2002). The community of practice additionally entails the process of social learning that takes place when individuals who have common interests in some field or problem collaborate and share ideas, come up with solutions and otherwise interact with each other to work (Saint-Onge and Wallace 2003; Hildreth and Kimble 2004).

It constitutes a very attractive arrangement for many undertakings as nothing binds people together faster than common interest and pursuit of solutions to common problems (Wenger 1998; Wenger et al. 2002; Saint-Onge and Wallace 2003; Hildreth and Kimble 2004). The idea that successful learning of any skill, body of knowledge, or developing expertise or proficiency in some field involves a route in which participation and involvement play a key role has gained significant ground in recent years. Communities of practice have been seen as an arrangement in which such more profound and therefore more insightful participation is possible. They have an additional value of regulating internal organization and development of internal structure for various collective and collaborative ventures, where such structure is difficult to conceive from the very start of the endeavour as solutions, as well as new concerns and issues to deal with, are often generated en route. This is succinctly captured in the words of McDermott below:

> Learning traditionally gets measured on the assumption that it is a possession of individuals that can be found inside their heads. By [this] approach learning is in the relationships between people. Learning is in the conditions that bring people together and organize a point of contact that allows for particular pieces of information to take on a relevance; without the points of contact, without the system of relevancies, there is no learning, and there is little memory. Learning does not belong to individual persons, but to the various conversations of which they are a part.
>
> (McDermott 1999:16)

Within the scenario assessment tool, the role of a community of practice is twofold. On the one hand, it is through collaborative work, exchange of ideas and trying to capture the essence of what makes people culturally different that the scenarios are created. On the other hand, the collaborative efforts of the members of the community allow both the assessment of the communicative language ability as well as the assessment of intercultural communication competences to happen. Through this joint, collaborative and communal process, the people who enter the assessment procedure of their performance focus on various aspects of it, as seen through the perspective of the CoP and through self-assessment INCA scales, have the opportunity for reflective activities concerning their own communication and performance, attitudes, beliefs and the degree of their open-mindedness.

6. Reflection in developing strategic competence in communication in professional settings via the Web

The existence of a community seems to be one of the prerequisites in stimulating reflection on language use in professional contexts. Interactions with other members of the community of practice may encourage the learner to re-examine, and reflect on, the kinds and types of one's own behaviour and practice with regard to the various differences between cultures and the tendency to rely on one's ethnocentrism in intercultural encounters with members of other cultures. However, the fact that there is a forum where collaborative efforts at examining task performance result in discourse whose participants trust each other to have their behaviour scrutinised, examined in minute detail and assessed with extensive comments, while being a prerequisite, is yet sufficient for reflection. Awareness of what constitutes successful communication and the ability to identify when the conditions for it are being violated seems to play a significant role (Byram 1997).

This awareness and the ability to reflect on experiences at hand may be developed via exposure to various aspects of a communication instance through the Web-based scenario tool of the CEFcult environment. When the differences between one's own culture and the cultures of the other participants of the discourse are too small to acknowledge, but large enough to result in different understanding of what is being conveyed, the participants tend to ignore them as it is only natural to assume that any instance of communication is essentially laced with potential misunderstandings. This is true even if the participants come from the same ideosphere and share their mimetic behavioural paradigms, because meaning in communication is not given but needs to be negotiated and sometimes explicated (Krakowian 2011a, b). The scenarios may be constructed in such a way that they exaggerate some of the differences or make them the focal point of attention in order to make them sufficiently apparent, explicit and obvious.

The added bonus of all of this happening online and in a CoP of like-minded individuals is that the simulated experience is safe, has a face-saving quality and may be effected as many times as necessary, and at no additional affective cost. The scaffolding of experience through observing how ideas are shared in the Community of Practice is another advantage as learners most commonly need to develop reflective skills from scratch (Schön 1990). The path to reflection in a moderated, open community where the pursuit of common goals encourages diversity of opinion rather than one version of the truth starts from guided reflection prompted by social interactions, and in due course leads to the ability to critically observe one's own action from different points of view and different perspectives.

With the use of available tools and mechanisms accessible online at the discretion of the end user, the path from lack of awareness, through noticing, understanding, empathising and finally being able to assume another person's perspective can be dramatically shortened owing to the sheer accumulation of experience under conducive circumstances. There is little doubt in the author's mind that this and similar technologies may be used to coach users to develop their reflective skills of acknowledging, appreciating and assuming other people's perspectives when communicating across cultures.

7. Concluding remarks

There are at least two advantages of using the Web-based application as an assessment tool in evaluating intercultural communication that immediately spring to mind. The first of these is the collaborative nature of the assessment tool. Instead of drawing on the type of assessment where an aspiring user is faced with an assessment rendered by an anonymous expert of sorts, the tool offers an environment where end-users, their peers, instructors or, in fact, any other interested parties can compare their appraisal of the user's performance on a scenario, all of which can be considered a valuable mode of providing feedback with the potential to trigger reflective thinking, the added value being here in diminishing anxiety and providing scaffolding instrumental in developing reflective skills. The second advantage lies in the customisation nature of the assessment tool as the platform allows tailor-made scenarios and scenario adaptations to be created with the use of the scenario builder, so they can be adapted to fit specific needs and situations.

There are numerous potential applications of the assessment tool outlined in the preceding sections. From training employees to recognising issues in communicating in multicultural professional settings, to creating portfolios of interaction with various prompts in the form of more or less complex and extended scenarios. One attractive option to be derived from a system like this might be in low stakes certification and confirmation of skills, if an export facility were to be linked to portals such as LinkedIn®, BranchOut®, VisualCV® and other. Then there is, obviously, the benefit of developing the ability to self-reflect that was discussed, which, by any means, can be seen as superior to any other advantages to be derived from the tool, its scenarios and the CoP it entails.

References

Byram, Michael
1997 *Teaching and Assessing Intercultural Communicative Competence*. Clevedon: Multilingual Matters.

Byram, Michael – Bella Gribkova – Hugh Starkey
2002 *Developing the Intercultural Dimension in Language Teaching. A Practical Introduction for Teachers*. Strasbourg: Council of Europe.

Council of Europe (COE)
2001 *Common European Framework of Reference for Languages: Learning, Teaching, Assessment*. Cambridge: Cambridge University Press.

Council of Europe (COE)
2008 *White Paper on Intercultural Dialogue – Living Together As Equals in Dignity* retrieved from http://www.coe.int/t/dg4/intercultural/publication_whitepaper_id_EN.asp

Hildreth, Paul M. – Chris Kimble
2004 *Knowledge Networks: Innovation through Communities of Practice*. Hershey, London: Idea Group Inc.

Krakowian, Przemysław
2011a *Investigating Rater Behaviour in Tests of Oral Expression.* Łódź: Łódź University Press.
2011b "Transcultural interference, Communities of Practice and collaborative assessment of oral performance", in Mirosław Pawlak - Ewa Waniek-Klimczak - Jan Majer (eds.), 300–311.

Lustig, Myron W. – Jolene Koester
1999 *Intercultural Competence: Interpersonal Communication across Cultures.* New York: Longman.

McDermott, Richard P.
1999 "On becoming labelled – the story of Adam", in Patricia Murphy (ed.), 1–21.

Murphy, Patricia. (ed.)
1999 *Learners, Learning and Assessment.* London: Paul Chapman Publishing (SAGE) in association with The Open University.

Pawlak, Mirosław – Ewa Waniek-Klimczak – Jan Majer (eds.)
2011 *Speaking and Instructed Foreign Language Acquisition.* Clevedon: Multilingual Matters.

Saint-Onge, Hubert – Debra Wallace
2003 *Leveraging Communities of Practice.* Burlington: Butterworth Heinemann.

Schön, Donald A.
1990 *Educating the Reflective Practitioner.* San Francisco: Jossey-Bass.

Sheils, Joe
1988 *Communication in the Modern Language Classroom.* Strasbourg: Council of Europe.

Wenger, Etienne
1998 *Communities of Practice: Learning, Meaning, and Identity.* Cambridge: Cambridge University Press.

Wenger, Etienne – Richard McDermott – William M. Snyder
2002 *Cultivating Communities of Practice.* Boston: HBS Press.

Mariusz Kruk
University of Zielona Góra, Zielona Góra, Poland

The Impact of Using Internet Resources and Browser-based Virtual Worlds on the Level of Foreign Language Anxiety

Abstract
This chapter reports the findings of a classroom-based study whose main purpose was to investigate the impact of using Internet resources and a browser-based virtual world on foreign language anxiety levels among Polish senior high school students. Two groups, one treatment (n=13) and one control (n=14), participated in the research project. The intervention spanned the period of one week. The instruction in the treatment group was based on Internet resources and the browser-based virtual world *Yoowalk*, while the students in the control group followed their regular coursebook activities. The data were collected by means of the Foreign Language Classroom Anxiety Scale (Horwitz et al. 1986), administered before and after the treatment, and subjected to quantitative analysis. The results show that although the intervention had a limited impact on lowering foreign language anxiety among the treatment subjects, it made them less anxious with regard to communication apprehension.

Keywords: foreign language anxiety, Internet resources, browser-based virtual worlds

1. Introduction

Foreign language anxiety has been recognized as one of the main obstacles to successful foreign language teaching and learning (Dewaele et al. 2008). It has frequently been attributed to language learners' inability to present their ideas or thoughts in the target language. Such a situation might result in diminishing students' self-esteem and weakening their self-image (Horwitz et al. 1986). Anxious language learners are often unable to pronounce words correctly while speaking or to create grammatically correct output. Students who experience language anxiety become confused and embarrassed in the language classroom, and, as a result, they are incapable of understanding written and spoken input. Furthermore, high levels of language anxiety may result in students' negative assessment of themselves or negative evaluation by others. All of this can contribute to turning foreign language learning into a particularly unpleasant experience for language learners (Horwitz and Young 1991; Horwitz 2001; Young 1999). It is, thus, not surprising that researchers and practitioners have been making efforts to comprehend the construct as well as seek ways in which to reduce levels of language anxiety. One such way may concern the implementation of modern technology in foreign language lessons. For example, language teachers should be open to the use of the Internet and virtual worlds during lessons. This type of openness may not only allow language learners to become more independent and interested in language learning but also make them more confident and willing to use the target language. It is unfortunate, however, that few research projects have taken into account the effects of implementing online resources and virtual worlds on lowering language learners' anxiety in foreign language teaching and learning. The study whose results are reported below represents an attempt to investigate the impact of using Internet resources and the browser-based virtual world *Yoowalk* in order to lower foreign language anxiety levels in a class of Polish senior high schools students.

2. Review of literature

2.1. Language anxiety

Similarly to other affective variables such as attitudes and motivation, for many decades anxiety has been studied as a potential factor influencing foreign language learning success. In general, anxiety can be viewed as "(…) the subjective feeling of tension, apprehension, nervousness, and worry associated with an arousal of the autonomic nervous system" (Spielberger 1983: 15). However, in the context of language learning, anxiety can be described as the feeling of tension and apprehension (MacIntyre and Gardner 1994), or, as a "(…) distinct complex of self-perceptions, beliefs, feelings, and behaviours related to classroom language learning arising from the uniqueness of the language learning process" (Horwitz et al. 1986: 128).

Language anxiety is seen as a situation-specific anxiety linked with the language learning context, which suggests that it "(…) can play a significant causal role in creating individual differences in language learning" (Tallon 2011: 75). Since "(…) foreign language anxiety concerns performance evaluation within an academic and social context" (Horwitz et al. 1986: 127), researchers draw parallels between it and three related performance anxieties: communication apprehension, fear of negative social evaluation and test anxiety. Communication apprehension arises from students' incapacity to adequately convey their thoughts. This is a type of shyness described by fear of or worry about communicating with other people. Fear of negative social evaluation is related to students' apprehension about being evaluated in various situations or avoidance of evaluative situations. Finally, test anxiety concerns worries and nervousness about academic evaluation or the fear of failure (Horwitz et al. 1986).

Young (1991) argues that language anxiety can be caused by: (1) personal and interpersonal anxiety, (2) learner beliefs about language learning, (3) teacher beliefs about language teaching, (4) teacher-learner interactions, (5) classroom procedures and (6) testing. It should also be added that research on anxiety distinguishes between facilitative anxiety, i.e. a positive impact on foreign language learning, and debilitative anxiety, which is a negative effect on foreign language learning (Alpert and Haber 1960; Ellis 2008; Scovel 1978). What is more, the level of task difficulty may affect students, who can develop facilitating or debilitating anxiety (MacIntyre 1995: 92).

2.2. Empirical research into language anxiety

Of interest to the present study are attempts to account for the relationship between anxiety and computer aided language learning. For example, Majid et al. (2012) conducted a questionnaire study among 57 adult learners who attended an online language course. The study sought to determine the online language learning anxiety as well as to identify the relationship between different domains of online language learning anxiety. By and large, the results demonstrated that the learners were not anxious while studying the target language online. However, Majid et al. (2012) identified some areas of concern which comprised the learners' cognitive ability in understanding the processes involved in online language learning and the subjects' fear of attending such courses. The researchers found significant relationship between the students' readiness and confidence, experience and motivation as well as attributes and confidence.

In another study, Aydin (2011) investigated Internet anxiety among foreign language learners in order to determine the relationships between Internet anxiety and certain variables. A sample of 115 students completed a background questionnaire, an Internet information test and an Internet anxiety scale. The results showed that the Internet was not in itself a source of anxiety among the subjects but it was the situations in which the students had to use the Internet that led to Internet anxiety. In addition, the researcher observed that gender, computer and Internet connectivity, Internet instruction, familiarity with the Internet and information level significantly correlated with the level of Internet anxiety.

Yet another interesting contribution to research on language anxiety and the use of modern technology was the research project undertaken by Chuo (2007), who investigated the effects of the WebQuest Writing Instruction program on

Taiwanese EFL students' writing development, writing apprehension and perception of Web-resource integrated language learning. The results of the study demonstrated that students in the online writing class improved their writing significantly more than those in the conventional classroom writing class. The students who received innovative treatment significantly reduced their writing apprehension. It has to be added, however, that no significant difference in reduced apprehension was found between the two groups. Although no significant correlation was observed between the subjects' perception and their improved writing performance, the learners pointed to a large number of benefits concerning learning by means of online resources.

It is also necesary to mention the research projects carried out by Plastina (2005) and Ward (2004). Plastina investigated whether situational anxiety could be superseded by virtual learning environments (VLEs) and concluded that "(…) the VLEs tend to reduce this form of anxiety in the majority of dominant introvert personality types although in different ways. The specificity of different VLEs and their pedagogical purpose besides learners' age and technological skills strongly influence virtual behavior" (Plastina 2005: 130). As for the other study, Ward found out that writing a blog is communicative, provides language learners with an audience for their texts and reduces anxiety.

There have been many attempts to account for the fact that computer-mediated communication (CMC) can lower foreign language anxiety. Arnold (2007), for example, looked into the relationship between CMC and communication apprehension. The study spanned one term and involved 56 students of German who participated in group discussions. The control group completed the discussions face-to-face while the experimental groups used synchronous and asynchronous computer-mediated communication. The results showed no significant difference in the level of communication apprehension between the control and the experimental groups. On the other hand, the study carried out by Freiermuth and Jarrell (2006) employed questionnaires and analysis of the discourse produced by small groups of female Japanese university students. The groups were requested to solve language tasks in both the online and the traditional face-to-face setting, and the results demonstrated that chatting in the target language with non-native speakers of English reduced anxiety, improved output and increased learner control.

Research into virtual worlds and their effects on foreign language anxiety is still in its infancy due to the novelty of these new learning environments. According to Peterson (2011), the anonymity factor offered by virtual worlds can reduce anxiety and produce a stress-free setting for language learners. Grant et al. (2013) in their research project compared foreign learner anxiety in an online multi-user 3D virtual world simulation with the real-world classroom. The results showed that the subjects found the virtual environment less stressful when it came to language use. In addition, Balcikanli (2012) reported experiences of two groups of students, seven American students learning Turkish as a foreign language in the USA and eight Turkish learners studying English in Turkey, in the Second Life environment. His findings revealed that Second Life offered a less threatening learning environment for the subjects. Yet another study (Wehner et al. 2011) looked at how the use of Second Life impacted the motivation of students of the Spanish language. The students were divided into two groups. One group utilized Second Life as part of their curriculum, while the other group received traditional instruction. Basing on the results obtained, the researchers concluded that virtual worlds may be a factor in both reducing language anxiety and increasing their motivation to learn the target language. Quite interesting are also the results of the study carried out by Jauregi (2011), who tried to find added value in integrating synchronous collaboration projects through video-communication or Second Life in language instruction. By comparing two groups of students, an experimental Second Life and Web-video-communication group and a control group of students taking regular lessons, the researcher found "(…) significant differences for perceived competence in the target language, positive attitudes towards talking to native speakers, and decrease of speaking anxiety" (Jauregi 2011: 77).

Given the importance attached to anxiety in second/foreign language teaching and learning, it may come as a surprise that little attention has been given to the relationship between this variable and a combination of online resources with virtual worlds. It is the belief of the present author that there is a clear need for more such research, and that was the main impulse for carrying out the study described below.

3. Study

3.1. Research questions

The main aim of the study was to investigate the use of Internet resources and a browser-based virtual world with a view to lowering foreign language anxiety levels in Polish senior high schools students. Specifically, the study sought to address the following research questions:

1. What levels of anxiety are reported by the participants before and after the intervention?
2. Does the use of online resources and the browser-based virtual world result in lowering foreign language anxiety?

3.2. Participants

The subjects were 27 third-grade senior high school students. They were aged 18–19 and were randomly divided into two groups: the treatment group (TG) (N=13) and the control group (CG) (N=14). It should be noted that such a division was consistent with the policy of the school, which is to divide class units of more than 25 students into smaller groups for foreign language lessons. In addition, each group had three hours of English per week. Prior to the treatment procedure, the subjects were requested to fill in a questionnaire whose aim was to provide background information related to the learners' personal history of foreign language learning, attitudes, motivations and access to the Internet. The analysis of the responses revealed that, on average, the learners in TG had been learning English for 8.46 years and the students in CG for 8.50 years. Despite this fact, the students could be said to have represented a pre-intermediate level of proficiency and most of them had a rather weak command of English. As regards their grades, the grade point average in English at the end of the second class amounted to 2.38 and 2.57 on a 0–6 scale for TG and CG, respectively. This shows that the groups were comparable and the learning outcomes were poor. In addition, the subjects' self-assessment turned out to be slightly higher in TG than in CG and equalled 2.77 and 2.50, respectively. All the subjects stated that they had access to the Internet at home; however, they used it only occasionally to study English. When asked about the subjects' most favourite elements of English, the majority of them indicated vocabulary (62 % →TG and 71 % → CG). The students considered grammar to be the most difficult for them to study (85 % → TG and 64 % → CG). Finally, the treatment students reported a higher level of anxiety at the beginning of the study when compared with the control students (see Table 1).

Table 1. The participants of the study

	Treatment group (TG)	**Control group (CG)**
Number of students	13	14
Number of English lessons per week	3	
The length of English language learning experience (average in years)	8.46	8.50
The level of competence	A2 (according to the *Common European Framework of Reference for Languages*)	
The grade point average	2.38	2.57
The level of anxiety at the beginning of the study	3.32	3.07

3.3. Research schedule

Table 2 provides the details of the research schedule. The Foreign Language Classroom Anxiety Scale (FLCAS) and the background questionnaire were filled in by the subjects one week prior to the treatment in order to establish the initial levels of foreign language anxiety. The same scale was administered again one and four weeks after the treatment to provide information related to the impact of the treatment on the levels of anxiety right after the intervention and after the period of several weeks.

Table 2. Research schedule

Week	Procedure
Week 1	Foreign Language Classroom Anxiety Scale (FLCAS1) and background questionnaire
Week 2	Treatment (three 45-minute lessons)
Week 3	Foreign Language Classroom Anxiety Scale (FLCAS2)
Week 4–6	Regular lessons
Week 7	Foreign Language Classroom Anxiety Scale (FLCAS3)

3.4. Treatment

As regards the students in the treatment group, the first lesson began with the students searching the Internet and using Web pages of their own choice to find information related to the Past Simple tense. They were requested to take notes on the use of the structure in question, sentence formation and examples of positive and negative sentences as well as questions. The second half of the class was devoted to grammar practice. Thus, the learners were provided with links to several websites which contained a variety of exercises on the Past Simple tense.[1] The learners were asked to choose and perform several activities of the following types: writing sentences with the use of given words, answering questions, rewriting sentences, filling the gaps, matching and asking about the underlined part of the sentence.

1 For example, http://www.ego4u.com/en/cram-up/grammar/simple-past#exercises, http://www.english-grammar-lessons.com/pastsimple/menu.php, http://www.ang.pl/cwiczenia/gramatyka/past_simple, http://perso.wanadoo.es/autoenglish/gr.pastsim.i.htm

The second lesson commenced with further grammar practice by means of the above-mentioned websites and activities. After approximately twenty minutes, the students were requested to log on to the browser-based virtual world *Yoowalk* (http://www.yoowalk.com/)[2] in order to talk with the residents of this virtual reality, i.e. the students of their own group. It must be added that the students were requested to ask questions in the Past Simple tense and provide full answers. With regards to the last lesson, it was in its entirety conducted in the virtual world. Here again, the subjects were requested to use the grammar item in question in order to collect relevant data to write a short report.[3] It has to be noted that the activities in the virtual world allowed the treatment students to use the grammar structure in practice.

The first lesson conducted in the control group started with the teacher's presentation of the use, sentence formation and relevant examples related to the Past Simple tense and the students were told to write everything down in their notebooks. The remaining part of this lesson was devoted to doing a series of exercises from their coursebook (i.e. completing the sentences with the verbs in the correct form and rewriting sentences). The second class began with a simple gap filling activity. The exercise was checked by the teacher who asked at random several students to read their answers and then wrote the students' responses down on the board. During the next activity, the teacher asked each student questions which required them to provide short answers. This activity was followed by a similar task; however, this time the answers to the teachers' questions were to be answered in full sentences. The lesson finished with the students asking and answering various types of questions. It must be observed that the activities were supervised by the teacher, who always corrected the students' mistakes and provided feedback. As for the third lesson, it started with a short exercise in which the students were requested to write sentences from words in brackets. The activity was again checked by the teacher who nomi-

2 *Yoowalk* is a virtual representation of the World Wide Web consisting of *walksites,* i.e. categorized villages of 3D websites, that users can browse with their avatars. *Yoowalk* offers synchronous text-based communication, it is very simple to navigate, provides anonymity and does not require its users to register in order to use it. *Yoowalk* was chosen due to low technical requirements and a slow Internet connection at the school in question.

3 The students were asked to perform the following activity: *You are working for a local newspaper. The editor asked you to write a short note on what local people did and didn't do last weekend, last week, last month and during last vacation. Ask as many people as possible, make notes and then write the note.*

nated several students to read and write the correct sentences on the board. As in the case of the third lesson conducted in the treatment group, the control students performed a similar activity. The students were asked to work in pairs, impersonate citizens of an imagined local town and use the Past Simple tense to obtain relevant information needed to write a short note on the residents' past activities.

3.5. Instruments of data collection

The Foreign Language Classroom Anxiety Scale (FLCAS) developed by Horwitz et al. (1986) (see Appendix) was utilized to assess the degree to which the participants of the study felt anxious in a foreign language classroom. It has to be noted that, although there are other instruments available for measuring the level of anxiety, such as input processing and output anxiety scales (MacIntyre and Gardner 1994) (cf. Ellis 2008: 693), FLCAS is a well-known and frequently used tool, the validity and reliability of which has long been recognized. The questionnaire includes 33 statements in the form of a Likert scale ranging from 1 (strongly agree) to 5 (strongly disagree). Although Horwitz et al. (1986) have never offered a model for component analysis for FLCAS, some researchers (e.g. Aida 1994) have proposed and utilized several component analysis models in their investigations. This study uses the model applied in the study conducted by Briesmaster and Briesmaster-Paredes (2015), in which the statements are intended to tap the following components: communication apprehension (e.g. "I start to panic when I have to speak without preparation in language class."), test anxiety (e.g. "I worry about the consequences of failing my language class.") and fear of negative evaluation (e.g. "I am afraid that the other students in the class will laugh at me when I speak in English."). It must be added that the negatively worded statements were reversed and recoded so that in all instances a high score represented high foreign language anxiety (cf. Briesmaster and Briesmaster-Paredes 2015). Taking into account the participants' low level of proficiency, and to avoid potential misunderstandings, the original version of the questionnaire was translated into Polish. It should also be pointed out that the Polish version of the instrument had been piloted with learners who did not participate in the research project. In addition to FLCAS, all the participants filled in the background questionnaire which queried them about the length of their English instruction, their out-of-class exposure to the target language and other issues which could potentially prove useful while interpreting the findings of the study.

3.6. Data analyses

The scale of the Polish version of FLCAS has been shown to be both reliable and valid each time it was administered, with the lowest alpha coefficient of .89 and the highest of .95 (the average amounted to .92). In addition, the analyses involved tabulating the means, ranges and standard deviations for the whole instrument. Since some of the data obtained were not normally distributed, the levels of statistical significance were established by means of the nonparametric Wilcoxon Signed-Ranks Test and the Mann-Whitney U Test. The former was used to detect changes in the degree of foreign language anxiety of one group on FLCAS, and the latter was employed when the treatment and control groups were compared.

3.7. Results and discussion

As evidenced by the data presented in Table 3, the students in the control group (CG) reported lower levels of anxiety at the beginning of the study when compared with the learners in the treatment group (TG). It should be noted, however, that the difference in the means between the groups on FLCAS1 amounted to 0.25 and was not statistically significant ($U = 398$, $p = 0.060$). The situation looked different immediately after the intervention (FLCAS2) and after four weeks (FLCAS3), with CG showing more anxiety when compared to TG. However, the difference in the means between the groups on FLCAS2 and FLCAS3 was minute (0.05 and 0.01, respectively) and did not reveal statistical significance ($U = 535$, $p = 0.90$ and $U = 505$, $p = 0.617$, respectively). The analysis of the data also showed that the intervention did not result in a statistically significant change in the treatment students' levels of anxiety each time the FLCAS was administered ($p > 0.05$) (see Table 3). As for CG, the differences between the means of FLCAS1-FLCAS2 and FLCAS1-FLCAS3 were quite substantial; they amounted to 0.27 and 0.25, respectively and turned out to be statistically significant (see Table 3). Such outcomes may testify to a limited impact of Internet resources and the virtual world *Yoowalk* on the treatment students' anxiety levels in English lessons. However, given the design of the study, i.e. small sample and class sizes, such a conclusion may only be tentative.

Table 3. Means, standard deviations, ranges and statistical significance on FLCAS for TG and CG

	Treatment group (TG)			Control group (CG)		
	FLCAS1	FLCAS2	FLCAS3	FLCAS1	FLCAS2	FLCAS3
Mean	3.32	3.29	3.31	3.07	3.34	3.32
Standard deviation	.58	.48	.53	.55	.39	.36
Range	2.23	1.92	1.85	2.10	1.42	1.50
Significance (two tailed Wilcoxon test)	FLCAS1→FLCAS2 $Z = -.517, p = .605$ FLCAS2→FLCAS3 $Z = -.309, p = .757$ FLCAS1→FLCAS3 $Z = -.337, p = .736$			FLCAS1→FLCAS2 $Z = -2.806, p = .005$* FLCAS2→FLCAS3 $Z = -.375, p = .707$ FLCAS1→FLCAS3 $Z = -2.440, p = .015$*		

Although the overall results of FLCAS demonstrated that both groups reported high levels of anxiety each time the instrument was used, the data included in Table 3 indicate that there were some changes in the values of the standard deviation and the range in TG, with the former dropping by 0.10 points and the latter decreasing by 0.31 points from FLCAS1 to FLCAS2. It should be noted, however, that the changes in the values of the measures of dispersion were more visible in CG, with the values of the standard deviation dropping by 0.16 points and the range decreasing by 0.68 from FLCAS1 to FLCAS2. Such results might suggest that, on the whole, the intervention had a rather limited effect on diminishing individual variation in terms of anxiety levels in TG.

Table 4 and Table 5 below present the number of items with lower and higher means for the three components of FLCAS in both groups. It is important to note that immediately after the intervention (FLCAS2) the treatment students showed less communication apprehension and fear of negative evaluation. They also experienced somewhat lower levels of test anxiety and fear of negative evaluation on FLCAS3 when compared with FLCAS1. As for the control learners, they became more anxious on FLCAS2 in the areas of communication apprehension and fear of negative evaluation as well as in test anxiety and fear of negative evaluation on FLCAS3. A possible explanation of these findings might be related to stress-free learning conditions created by the Internet-based environment, which allowed students to work at their own pace and without constant – and, for some students, stressful – control of the teacher. It has to be remembered, however, that such conclusions can only be tentative, given – among other things – the slight differences in student numbers between the groups, the small sample size and the short time span of the study.

Table 4. Number of items with lower means for the three components of FLCAS in TG and CG

	Treatment group (TG)			Control group (CG)		
	FLCAS1	FLCAS2	FLCAS3	FLCAS1	FLCAS2	FLCAS3
Communication apprehension	1	5	1	10	6	10
Test anxiety	9	9	10	6	6	5
Fear of negative evaluation	2	4	4	5	3	3

Table 5. Number of items with higher means for the three components of FLCAS in TG and CG

	Treatment group (TG)			Control group (CG)		
	FLCAS1	FLCAS2	FLCAS3	FLCAS1	FLCAS2	FLCAS3
Communication apprehension	10	6	10	1	5	1
Test anxiety	6	6	5	9	9	10
Fear of negative evaluation	5	3	3	2	4	4

The analysis of the data revealed that the treatment subjects' level of foreign language anxiety lowered immediately after the intervention (FLCAS2) when compared with FLCAS1 in as many as 13 items (i.e. items 1, 4, 7, 8, 10, 14, 15, 18, 25, 29, 30, 32 and 33). In addition, two differences in the means displayed statistical significance: item 10 "I worry about the consequences of failing my language class" ($Z = -1.994$, $p = 0.046$) and statement 25 "Language class moves so quickly I worry about getting left behind" ($Z = -2.111$, $p = 0.035$). It should also be pointed out that 6 statements (i.e. items 6, 11, 19, 22, 28 and 31) remained unchanged between FLCAS1 and FLCAS2 and two items (i.e. 1 and 28) decreased from FLCAS1 to FLCAS3. However, none of these differences displayed statistical significance ($p > 0.05$). In addition, the largest and statistically significant increase in the level of anxiety was observed from FLCAS1 to FLCAS2 and found in item 26 "I feel more tense and nervous in my language class than in my other classes" ($Z = -2.232$, $p = 0.026$). While such findings can be ascribed to the potentially anxiety-free digital environment that the students were allowed to participate in, the rise in the level of anxiety in statement 26 might be related to both the novelty of such environments and the students' independence in studying the target language during the lessons. As it was stated above, the treatment subjects became less anxious with regard to communication apprehension immediately after the intervention when compared with FLCAS1. However, the students' levels of communication apprehension rose again on FLCAS3 and became as high as on FLCAS1 (see Table 4 and Table 5). A possible explanation of this finding might be related to the fact that the treatment students found the opportunity to converse in the virtual world *Yoowalk* to be less stressful than conversations conducted in the target language in the conventional classroom. This is because *Yoowalk* offers more anonymity and, thus, the students may have felt more confident and relaxed.

It is also worth pointing out that the treatment subjects displayed quite low levels of test anxiety. This indicates that in this area the intervention did not make the subjects more anxious. This positive finding can be partly accounted for by the fact that the students could, for example, self-check and assess their own performance by choosing appropriate options available on some Web pages or, as indicated above, converse in a stress-free environment. This means that the treatment allowed the students to avoid potentially stressful situations related to teachers' evaluation of their work.

As regards the control subjects, the traditional treatment employed in this group resulted in lowering anxiety on FLCAS2 in ten items (i.e. 1, 3, 5, 6, 8, 22, 23, 28, 29 and 31). In addition, the students in CG showed less anxiety from FLCAS1 to FLCAS3 in items 5 and 8; however, these decreases did not prove to be statistically significant ($p > 0.05$). It has to be noted that the control learners manifested higher levels of anxiety: from FLCAS1 to FLCAS2 in item 19 ("I am afraid that my language teacher is ready to correct every mistake I make"); from FLCAS2 to FLCAS3 in item 6 ("During language class, I find myself thinking about things that have nothing to do with the course"); and from FLCAS1 to FLCAS3 in item 16 ("Even if I am well prepared for language class, I feel anxious about it"). What is more, these increases were substantial enough to the level of statistical significance ($Z = -2.414$, $p = 0.016$; $Z = -2.126$, $p = 0.033$ and $Z = -2.354$, $p = 0.019$, respectively).

It is interesting to note that, unlike the subjects in TG, the control students manifested higher levels of anxiety on FLCAS2 in test anxiety and fear of negative evaluation. On the other hand, however, the students felt less anxious in communication apprehension on FLCAS3 with the level of anxiety in this area being the same as on FLCAS1 (see Tables 4 and 5). Such results demonstrate that traditional instruction, which favours the teacher and gives him or her the power to evaluate students' progress, did little to lower the level of the control students' foreign language anxiety and, in fact, made them even more anxious.

4. Conclusions

The analysis of the data demonstrated that the treatment subjects' levels of foreign language anxiety were lower after the intervention (i.e. on FLCAS2 and FLCAS3) when compared with the initial level (i.e. on FLCAS1); however, they were minute and not statistically significant. By contrast, the control learners' levels of foreign language anxiety were lower before the study and higher after it. In addition, some of the differences in the degree of anxiety between FLCAS in this group were statistically significant. It should also be noted that the differences in the levels of anxiety between the two groups turned out to be statistically significant each time the instrument was used. While there might be many reasons for such a state of affairs, one plausible explanation could lie in the fact that the treatment students exercised more freedom during the lessons in question. They were, for example, allowed to visit Internet pages and search for needed information of their own choice as well as choose activities to perform or a student with whom to converse in the virtual world. What is more, the treatment learners studied English without the constant control of the teacher. This may have made them more independent, and, at the same time, less stressed during these English classes. It has to be noted, however, that due to the small-scale study conducted over a short time span, the conclusion may only be tentative and should be treated with caution.

The beneficial effects of using Internet-based resources and virtual worlds are more pronounced in items reflective of communication apprehension. As the analysis of FLCAS showed, the treatment subjects manifested somewhat lower levels of communication apprehension immediately after the intervention, while the control learners became more anxious in this respect, at the same time. This finding may be explained in terms of anonymity offered by using avatars to communicate in virtual worlds as well as a chance to use the target language more willingly. What is more, the opportunity to hide behind their avatars may have played a part in making the subjects feel less susceptible to criticism and reducing the danger of being laughed at by their colleagues. Yet another explanation might be related to the treatment students' increased interest and engagement in activities and conversations in the virtual world.

The data gathered by means of the background questionnaire (see Subsection 3.2.) and observations demonstrated that the students involved in this study could best be described as weak. It should not be surprising, then, that the learners in both groups manifested quite high levels of anxiety, which is consistent with the results of other research projects that showed that weaker students display higher levels of anxiety (c.f. Ellis 2008). As noted above, however, the results of the study revealed that the instruction employed in TG contributed to a somewhat lower level of foreign language anxiety among the students in this group. This may indicate that the use of online-based resources and virtual environments might have had a beneficial effect on reducing foreign language anxiety, at least when it comes to the participants of this study.

The main strengths of the study reported in this paper are connected with the fact that it was classroom-based and involved one intact class performing online and virtual world-based activities as well as traditional exercises as part of their regularly scheduled instruction. Nonetheless, the study also suffers from some limitations that should be addressed in future empirical investigations of this type.

Firstly, the period of one week during which three 45-minute lessons were conducted is too short and longitudinal studies are necessary to produce and capture the effect of implementing a combination of online resources and virtual environments on lessening foreign language anxiety.

Secondly, the subjects were required to fill in the same questionnaire three times and answer the same questions in a relatively short time, which may have potentially resulted in boredom or produced unreliable data.

In addition to quantitative data collection tools, qualitative data should also be implemented in order to collect rich data and analyse them from different angles and perspectives, especially while dealing with small samples of subjects and limited numbers of foreign language classes.

Finally, and most importantly perhaps, the small number of participants considerably reduces the generalizability of the results. Thus, future studies should involve larger samples and students of different levels of target language proficiency as well as diverse educational levels.

Despite these limitations and weaknesses, which should no doubt be taken into consideration when planning future empirical investigations, the study might still contribute to the knowledge of anxiety in foreign language learning. It should also be emphasized that better understanding of the concept of foreign language anxiety can assist language teachers in choosing techniques and teaching resources to reduce the feeling of tension and nervousness in specific groups of learners as well as situations, and, thus, making the whole process of foreign language learning more enjoyable and effective.

References

Aida, Yukie
1994 "Examination of Horwitz, Horwitz, and Cope's construct of foreign language anxiety: The case of students of Japanese", *Modern Language Journal, 78*(2), 155–168.

Alpert, Richard – Ralph N. Haber
1960 "Anxiety in academic achievement situations", *Journal of Abnormal and Social Psychology, 61*, 207–215.

Arnold, Nike
2007 "Reducing foreign language communication apprehension with computer-mediated communication: A preliminary study", *System, 35*, 469–486.

Aydin, Selami
2011 "Internet anxiety among foreign language learners", *TechTrends: Linking Research and Practice to Improve Learning, 55*(2), 46–54.

Balcikanli, Cem
2012 "Language learning in Second Life: American and Turkish students' experiences", *Turkish Online Journal of Distance Education-TOJDE, 13*(2), 131–146.

Briesmaster, Mark – Judith Briesmaster-Paredes
2015 "The relationship between teaching styles and NNPSETs' anxiety levels", *System, 49*, 145–156.

Chuo, Tun-Whei Isabel
2007 "The effects of the WebQuest writing instruction program on EFL learners' writing performance, writing apprehension, and perception", *TESL-EJ, 11*(3), 1–27.

Czepielewski, Sławomir (ed.)
2011 *Learning a Language in Virtual Worlds: A Review of Innovation and ICT in Language Teaching Methodology*. Warsaw: Warsaw Academy of Computer Science, Management and Administration.

Dewaele, Jean-Marc – Konstantinos V. Petrides – Adrian Furnham
2008 "The effects of trait emotional intelligence and sociobiographical variables on communicative anxiety and foreign language anxiety among adult multilinguals: A review and empirical investigation", *Language Learning 59*, 911–960.

Ellis, Rod
2008 *The Study of Second Language Acquisition*. Oxford: Oxford University Press.

Freiermuth, Mark – Douglas Jarrell
2006 "Willingness to communicate: Can on-line chat help?", *International Journal of Applied Linguistics, 16*(2), 190–213.

Grant, Scott John – Hui Huang – Sarah E. Pasfield-Neofitou
2013 "Language learning in virtual worlds: The role of foreign language and technical anxiety", *Journal of Virtual Worlds Research, 6*(1), 1–9.

Horwitz, Elanie K.
2001 "Language anxiety and achievement", *Annual Review of Applied Linguistics 21*, 112–126.

Horwitz, Elanie K. – Michael B. Horwitz – Joann Cope
1986 "Foreign language classroom anxiety", *The Modern Language Journal 70*(2), 125–132.

Horwitz, Elanie K. – Dolly J. Young (eds.)
1991 *Language Anxiety: From Theory and Research to Classroom Implications*. Englewood Cliffs, NJ: Prentice Hall.

Jauregi, Kristi
2011 "Integrating meaningful interactions through virtual tools in foreign language education: Looking at the added value", in Sławomir Czepielewski (ed.), 73–80.

MacIntyre, Peter D.
1995 "How does anxiety affect second language learning? A reply to Sparks and Ganschow", *Modern Language Journal, 79*(1), 90–99.

MacIntyre, Peter D. – Robert C. Gardner
1994 "The effects of induced anxiety on three stages of cognitive processing in computerized vocabulary learning", *Studies in Second Language Acquisition, 16*, 1–17.

Majid, Faizah A. – Wan Nurul Elia – Haslee Sharil – Johan Eddy Luaran – Fazyudi Ahmad Nadzri
2012 "A study on the on-line language learning anxiety among adult learners", *International Journal of e-Education, e-Business, e-Management and e-Learning, 2*(3), 187–192.

Peterson, Mark
2011 "Towards a research agenda for the use of three-dimensional virtual worlds in language learning", *CALICO Journal, 29*(1), 67–80.

Plastina, Anna Franca
2005 "Situational anxiety in L2 instruction: A case study on learner virtual behavior", *Estudios de Linguistica Inglesa Applicada, 6*, 115–133.

Scovel, Thomas
1978 "The effect of affect on foreign language learning: A review of the anxiety research", *Language Learning, 28*, 129–142.

Spielberger, Charles D.
1983 *Manual for the State-trait Anxiety Inventory*. Palo Alto, California: Consulting Psychological Press.

Tallon, Michael
2011 "Heritage speakers of Spanish and foreign language anxiety: A pilot study", *Texas Papers in Foreign Language Education, 15*(1), 70–87.

Ward, Jason M.
2004 "Blog assisted language learning (BALL): Push button publishing for the pupils", *TEFL Web Journal, 3*(1), 1–16.

Wehner, Amy K. – Andrew W. Gump – Steve Downey
2011 "The effects of Second Life on the motivation of undergraduate students learning a foreign language", *Computer Assisted Language Learning, 24*(3), 277–289.

Young, Dolly Jesusita
1991 "Creating a low-anxiety classroom environment: What does language anxiety research suggest?", *The Modern Language Journal, 75*, 426–439.

Young, Dolly Jesusita (ed.)
1999 *Affect in Foreign Language and Second Language Learning: A Practical Guide to Creating a Low-anxiety Classroom Atmosphere*. Boston: McGraw-Hill.

Appendix

Foreign Language Classroom Anxiety Scale (FLCAS)

1. I never feel quite sure of myself when I am speaking in English.
2. I don't worry about making mistakes in language class.
3. I tremble when I know that I'm going to be called on in language class.
4. It frightens me when I don't understand what the teacher is saying in the English language.
5. It wouldn't bother me at all to take more English language classes.
6. During language class, I find myself thinking about things that have nothing to do with the course.
7. I keep thinking that the other students are better at language than I am.
8. I am usually at ease (comfortable) during tests in my language class.
9. I start to panic when I have to speak without preparation in language class.
10. I worry about the consequences of failing my language class.
11. I don't understand why some people get so upset over language classes.
12. In language class, I can get so nervous I forget things I know.
13. It embarrasses me to volunteer answers in my language class.
14. I would not be nervous speaking the English language with native speakers.
15. I get upset when I don't understand what the teacher is correcting.
16. Even if I am well prepared for language class, I feel anxious about it.
17. I often feel like not going to my language class.
18. I feel confident when I speak in English in my language class.
19. I am afraid that my language teacher is ready to correct every mistake I make.
20. I can feel my heart pounding when I'm going to be called on in language class.
21. The more I study for a language test, the more confused I get.
22. I don't feel pressure to prepare very well for language class.
23. I always feel that the other students speak the English language better than I do.
24. I feel very self-conscious about speaking English in front of the other students.
25. Language class moves so quickly I worry about getting left behind.
26. I feel more tense and nervous in my language class than in my other classes.
27. I get nervous and confused when I am speaking in my language class.
28. When I'm on my way to language class, I feel very sure and relaxed.
29. I get nervous when I don't understand every word the language teacher says.
30. I feel overwhelmed by the number of rules you have to learn to speak the English language.
31. I am afraid that the other students in the class will laugh at me when I speak in English.
32. I would probably feel comfortable around native speakers of the English language.
33. I get nervous when the language teacher asks questions which I haven't prepared in advance.

(Horwitz et al. 1986: 129–130)

Anita Buczek-Zawiła
Pedagogical University, Kraków, Poland

Why Online Dictionaries (Plural) Make You More Open When Developing English Pronunciation Skills – Users' Self-reports

Abstract
Many online dictionaries apart from the meaning definition(s) incorporate some information on the pronunciation of the listed items, most often in the form of a recording made available for users to listen to and emulate. Others complement it with IPA transcription. Both types of hints are useful for learning the spoken form of individual words, yet they do not assist in developing fluent pronunciation and effortless comprehension of longer stretches of spoken text. To develop that, users need more comprehensive and versatile dictionary entries.

The paper ventures to establish the tendencies for choosing a particular online dictionary – or, as it transpires from the observations and users' reports, a combination of dictionaries – among advanced EFL speakers. With the growing competence in English, they become more open to ideas that underline the meaningfulness of attention paid equally to the meaning as well as to the form. The opinions forwarded in anonymous questionnaires indicate that a good online dictionary may be an asset in developing lexical knowledge as well as better pronunciation, making EFL learners more open and more aware dictionary users.

Keywords: online dictionaries, openness in education, pronunciation entries, user choices

1. Introduction

Among the plethora of online dictionaries available, some have acquired the status of clear favourites among users, most notably those which offer translations of items into the users' native tongue. A great many of those online resources incorporate some information on the pronunciation of the listed items, most often in the form of a recording made available for users to listen to and emulate (see https://www.diki.pl). Others, additionally, offer the IPA transcription (see *Oxford Advanced Learner's Dictionary Online, Cambridge Dictionaries Online, Collins Online*)[1]. Some still ignore the pronunciation aspect altogether. While both types

1 There are also resources which use spelling-based hints for pronunciation using English letter-sound values, not terribly helpful for EFL learners (cf. dictionary.reference.com)

of hints are undoubtedly useful for learning the spoken form of individual items, they do not normally assist in developing fluent pronunciation as well as effortless comprehension of longer stretches of spoken text. To achieve that, a working and practical knowledge of, among other things, the reduced variants of a number of grammatical words is needed. These simplifications, characteristically known as weak forms, are, arguably, one of the most important elements in the English spoken discourse, from both the comprehension and production perspective. Some dictionaries, to mention for example the *Oxford Advanced Learner's Dictionary* (http://www.oxfordlearnersdictionaries.com) or the *Cambridge Online* (http://dictionary.cambridge.org), actually introduce users to this aspect of speech. They list the reduced variant alongside the regular, strong pronunciation in the form of recording and transcription. The *Oxford* or the *Collins,* at the same time, categorise the weak form as the major variant of the item. This way, users immediately see the specificity of such items and recognize their contribution to communication. *Diki.pl* does not do that, but has an added bonus in the form of recordings of sample sentences or phrases for users to play and listen to. These audio files naturally incorporate weak forms as well. The very popular and possibly most widely known *Google Translate* (https://translate.google.pl) has recordings of individual lexical items only, though this feature seems to be frequently overlooked by learners, who concentrate specifically on the translations of looked-up items.

This paper ventures to establish the tendencies for choosing a particular online dictionary – or, as it transpires from the observations and users' reports, a combination of dictionaries – among advanced EFL speakers. These speakers are very much aware that the spoken form of words, or sentences, is an integral part of knowing them, just as is the words' meaning. Therefore, users need more comprehensive and versatile dictionary entries and are willing to give up their hitherto favoured resources in favour of new ones which will be more tailored to their changing needs.

It appears that with the growing competence in English they become more open to ideas that underline the meaningfulness of attention paid equally to the meaning as well as to the form. Therefore, alongside the need to expand their active and passive lexical stock, they also see the necessity of developing better pronunciation skills, as these are perceived to be essential in successful communication. Consequently, dictionary users begin to realise that old favourites may no longer be sufficiently satisfactory in terms of catering to their growing and changing needs.

The opinions forwarded by students in anonymous questionnaires indicate that a good online dictionary may be an asset when the need to examine the new meaning arises. At the same time, they admit that while taking proper care of this aspect of word knowledge, the same dictionary may not comfortably assist in trying to develop one's oral skills. The *one-size-fits-all* dictionary seems no longer a good option. If they want to improve their pronunciation – an idea that in itself requires an open outlook on learning a language – they need to look for other resources, even if that means using more than one dictionary, or a dictionary with a different or unfamiliar organization and presentation structure. It also transpires from their opinions that it is precisely the attention and care they wish to give to the spoken form that makes them look for new solutions and opt for new choices, thus making them more open and more aware dictionary users and foreign language learners.

2. What do we know about online dictionary use?

In recent years a growing interest and a significant rise in the use of online dictionaries by EFL learners have been observed. Students generally willingly use online resources. That happens despite the reservations frequently voiced by their teachers. The concerns centre around the challenges the use of such dictionaries creates, among them distraction from learning or participating in class activities, over-simplified explanations, low quality sound recordings or insufficiently illustrious examples of use provided for EFL learners (Dashtestani 2013). These potential problems are counterweighed by the benefits the users are offered: the possibility of conducting quick searches, input enhancement and recognition of different learning styles and strategies (Dashtestani 2013). The studies reviewed by Dashtestani (2013) reveal that students generally adopt positive attitudes towards the use of online dictionaries and perceive them as beneficial and facilitating their learning.

Müller-Spitzer and Koplenig (2014) underscore the dynamicity and flexibility of online dictionaries, especially in comparison to the static character of printed ones. These lexicographic resources make it possible for the same information to be presented in different ways and via different media and cross-references. They also observe a shift from the design orientation to purpose orientation of online dictionaries. They are frequently corpus-based and allow for the potential integration of multimedia components into their entries. These could be audio files illustrating the pronunciation of a word, a phrase or a whole sentence. Some may also feature collocation graphs visualising frequently occurring word combinations. There is a growing trend for collaborative compilations of the lexical or other referential material to be contributed to various websites. Another visible trend is seen in attempts to make the dictionary more user-friendly by providing a fast or customisable user interface.

However, the survey and the experiment reported in Müller-Spitzer and Koplenig (2014) both reveal that what lexicographers would like to achieve in their contributions may depart somewhat from the demands and expectations of ordinary users. The survey showed that when asked to rate and later personally rank ten selected characteristics of good online dictionaries the respondents opted for reliability of content as the single most important aspect of a good (online) dictionary, with other classical criteria of reference sources (up-to-date content, clarity) following closely. The characteristics connected uniquely with online dictionaries, such as adaptability and multimedia features, were rated and ranked rather low as relatively less (or un-)important. Table 1 summarizes the subjects' answers.

Table 1. Characteristics for the rating/ranking task and the outcome (compiled from Müller-Spitzer and Koplenig 2014: 147–149)

ASPECT	MEANING	RATING/RANKING OUTCOME
Adaptability	The user interface is customisable.	8
Clarity	The general structure of the website enables you to easily find the information you need.	2
Links to other dictionaries	The entries also contain links to other dictionaries.	7
Links to the corpus	The entries also contain links to the relevant collection of texts (corpus).	6
Suggestions for further browsing	The entries contain links to other entries you might find interesting.	9
Long-term accessibility	You can be certain of accessing the different entries by using the previous URL (i.e. Web address) for future reference.	5
Multimedia content	The online dictionary also contains multimedia files, e.g. visual and audio media.	10
Reliability of content	You can rely on the accuracy and authorship of the content.	1
Speed	There is hardly any delay when the pages are loaded.	4
Up-to-date content	Possible mistakes are corrected on a regular basis; new word entries and linguistic developments are regularly published online.	2

In the interpretation of the data the authors venture the claim that the *reliability of content* criterion should not be treated as a variable but as a constant of a good online dictionary. This preference for content-related reliability is hardly surprising, whereas the low appreciation of unique characteristics of online dictionaries is. That is why the authors complement their study with some experimental data relating specifically to more innovative features such as multimedia or adaptability. The decision is based on the assumption that at least some respondents are not used to online dictionaries incorporating those features and are therefore unable to assess whether or not they need such functions. When informed about several possible multimedia applications and some features of an adaptable online dictionary, the respondents began to evaluate their usefulness differently with labels such as such as 'important', 'beneficial' or 'helpful'. The learners or users can be said to be as yet insufficiently familiar with enough examples to appreciate such innovative possibilities and may need to be gradually convinced of the quality and usability of these features.

The multimedia aspect, most important in the context of the present study, is broken into three sub-fields: audio pronunciations (audio files, illustrating the pronunciation of a word, a phrase or a whole sentence), illustrations and collocation graphs. Of these, the audio pronunciations were appreciated the most, as most useful and beneficial. The subsequent claim, and one that is generally valid, is that users need to have an opportunity to actually use the many innovative features before they are at all able to judge their usefulness or importance meaningfully. Robert Lew (2012 as cited in Müller-Spitzer and Koplenig 2014) confirms the attractiveness of multimedia integration for users, especially audio recordings.

What transpires from available research on online dictionary use is that many such dictionaries are indeed frequently used and register high numbers of consultations, most notably with learner users, and characteristically of ages between 17 and 24. Some such resources offer very innovative search procedures (e.g. from meaning to word search), which are hardly ever used. Still, medium-specific enrichment with innovative elements is subordinated to reliable meaning reference.

One thing has become increasingly clear with time: more learners use online dictionaries than printed ones and they do it both for private and for professional purposes, especially for activities that are carried out frequently or that require active involvement, such as writing or translating (Koplenig and Müller-Spitzer 2014). Additionally, since electronic resources can be accessed on different devices, including notebooks, personal computers, tablets and mobile or smart phones, this device independence guarantees maximum efficiency and flexibility.

It is also to be expected that more and more online dictionary use will be observed in the specific context of EFL courses. Here Dashtestani (2013) reports on the learners' (and teachers') opinions that EFL students need training on how to use these dictionaries efficiently, they ought to be instructed on how to choose suitable online resources and use them effectively. Technology is, after all, supposed to be part of EFL courses, therefore students should feel that it is both interesting and useful.

The available accounts of research into dictionary use, according to Hulstijn and Atkins (1998) or Tono (2001), underline the methodological considerations. The authors stress the need for systematic study of the ways in which various variables interact when dictionary users consult the reference source with sufficiently complex information structure. Hulstijn and Atkins (1998: 7–9) identify seven major areas of such research and though their ideas related primarily to traditional printed dictionary use, they are repeated here since they seem to have a more universal scope and can be applied to online dictionaries too. The areas are as follows:

- The attitudes, needs, habits and preferences of dictionary users
- Text or word comprehension
- Text or word production
- Vocabulary learning
- Dictionary-related perfomance in testing
- Teaching dictionary skills
- Critical comparisons and reviews of dictionaries

Among these, of particular interest for the present paper are investigations into the needs and attitudes as well as examination of word and text production.

Observing dictionary use is a challenge due to the largely private and introspective nature of lexicographic consultation. Various protocols have been used: self-observation and self-reporting sheets or think-aloud protocols. There is also the concern for users' awareness of being observed (observer's paradox). This may affect the way in which they consult dictionaries as well as the willingness - and frequency - with which they do so (Lew 2014).

For examining the attitudes and preferences among dictionary users, survey tools are commonly applied. "Questionnaires are the most commonly used of the […] methods, probably because they are reasonably easy to handle, also in terms of the needed amount in order to meet the requirements of modern statistics" (Tarp 2014: 21).

Tono (2001: 67) defends the use of surveys in dictionary use research in the following manner:

> Surveys can find out what happens inside the users more directly than is possible by simple observation. Surveys can be large-scale or small-scale depending on the scope of the study. The collection of information typically involves one or more of the following data-gathering techniques: structured or semi-structured interviews, self-completion or postal questionnaires, standardised tests of attainment or performance, and attitude tests. It should be noted, however, that the findings are still 'indirect' in the sense that they only record what the users think happen as opposed to what actually happens. Most popular devices are interviews and questionnaires.

The specific research technique of a questionnaire requires a very careful structuring of the questions. Pasek and Krosnick (2010, as cited in Koplenig and Müller-Spitzer 2014) understand it as a form of interpersonal interaction which follows certain conversational standards. The questions then ought to be clear and relatively easy to answer, especially so if we wish to avoid confusing the respondents. It is not free from certain flaws, the most notable of which is the so-called statistical *halo-effect*, which essentially follows from the respondents answering intentionally the way they intuitively feel the researcher expects them to answer. Still, as an opinion-polling device, surveys have their merits, and that is why one such questionnaire was used in the present study, discussed in Section 4.

Even with the focus of the paper limited to certain aspects of online dictionary users' choices, an amalgam of contextual, pedagogical, linguistic and affective factors need to be taken into consideration. One of those factors must be the concept of openness in education.

3. Openness in education – education for openness

For several years now the philosophy of openness has affected the practices of teaching and learning. The basic tenant of education envisaged in this way is that it must be viewed as "an enterprise of sharing" (Wiley and Green 2012: 82) and such efficient sharing helps learners more effectively accomplish their personal goals. The fundamental claim behind this approach is the conviction that knowledge should be considered a common good and be accessible as openly as possible, resulting also in increasing and growing tolerance for different goals and explicit support for people trying to achieve them (Wiley 2016).

Wiley and Green (2012) observe that openness is actually impacting many areas of education, be it teaching, curriculum, textbooks, research policy and others. Peter and Deimann (2013) add here the technical and social characteristics and the nature of the resources. Postulates that seem to be particularly relevant for our investigations relate to creating opportunities to innovate in the teaching and learning and enabling better personalization of instruction. At the same time, a rise of interest in self-education and self-improvement is becoming more pronounced. These are to be achieved, among other things, through free and informal participation of individuals. The exact path that learners would choose to support their individual learning depends to a large extent on their access to a variety of freely-usable sources and their (trained) ability to select what is personally relevant to their learning needs.

Students nowadays need not only open teaching practices and open access to resources, but also raised open social consciousness (Peter and Deimann 2013). That means they need to be encouraged to explore the many varied facets of openness in the context of their own (higher) education, even if practised by only some of their tutors. Through that they should be able to apply open thinking to the practices used, and they should be open about the final outcome of the learning course. Essentially, each person should be ready to learn something different, even if it departs radically from the initial educator- or learner-specified goals. As Wiley and Green (2012: 88) put it, "(…) students are empowered to learn what they need/want to learn and the journey of learning is often more important than any predefined learning outcomes"[2]. Therefore they could benefit considerably both from openness in education and from education into openness.

The latter has become evident in the context of a specific resource use in a specific group of students. The resources are the freely available online dictionaries of English and other translation applications. The group consists of advanced EFL learners – students in the Department of English at the Pedagogical University in Kraków. The general educational context is that they are constantly encouraged to make their English language skills better, to become more efficient learners, to continuously improve the quality of performance as speakers – after all, they are trained to be future professionals working with English and through English. The *strife for perfection* ideals are communicated to them in a good number of classes, though through personal involvement of the tutors rather than the institution itself. They are warned to eschew any ideas of knowledge compartmentalization and static progression. The idea is that they need to acquire an understanding that where to find knowledge may be more important than answering how or what that knowledge encompasses (Duke et al. 2013). Yet, they and their educators feel that frequently they have to make do with suboptimal materials and resources. Therefore, they are instructed to

2 These statements essentially stem from the new educational philosophy of connectivism, which also regards openness as a commonly agreed on prerequisite (Siemens 2004; Duke et al. 2013).

keep an open mind both for the new skills and resources, and, ideally, to develop the critical ability to draw distinctions between important and unimportant information and innovation (Siemens 2004). Online dictionaries - which they prefer to use anyway – provide a perfect tool for such 'education into openness' training since they nourish free and individual learning. The study reported on in the next section examines the connection between the tool and the participants in the educational context.

4. Study: method, data presentation and discussion

The fundamental idea underpinning this study is that dictionaries are utility tools which are to meet special types of human needs, namely punctual information needs which specific types of users may have in specific types of situation (Tarp 2014). The specific need tackled here is the inclusion of the pronunciation portion in the lexical item entry in the English language online dictionaries.

The efficiency and satisfaction of dictionary users were probed routinely via questionnaires in the early days of interest in the user perspective on dictionary use (Lew 2014). Since these two aspects are the primary focus of the present investigations, the study follows the well-established procedure of survey examination.

4.1. The method

The survey format in the form of a postal (via electronic channels) questionnaire was used to meet the demand for reliable empirical information on how online dictionaries are actually being used. It constitutes a part of a small-scale interpretative research, which is non-statistical and may suffer from some occasional subjectivity. It aims to investigate both actions and meaning of them, complemented by identifying the causes behind those actions.

The actual questionnaire consisted of 10 questions, some of them open, others closed. It required respondents to self-reflect on their practices of finding a particular application and using it in their personal study. Moreover, it was meant as an introductory part to a more extensive research into the effectiveness of pronunciation features in dictionaries in pronunciation training of their users.

Fifty-three subjects eventually filled in the survey and sent it back, all of them were freshmen students in the English Studies Department in Kraków, among them 32 were day students, and 21 were extramural ones. The reasons behind choosing this particular group are connected with aspects such as age (19–21 – save a few cases among the extramurals), command of English (above the FCE level) and being tech-comfy (at a minimum) to tech-savvy. It may therefore be assumed that they fall into the group of keen online dictionary users, unafraid of new technological appliances and constantly working on developing their English language skills.

The data obtained through this survey are presented and discussed in the following sections.

4.2. Data presentation

This section reports on the data extrapolated from the questionnaire filled in by fifty-three respondents. The form began with a very general question *What type of English language dictionary do you use in college or for home study?* The aim was to establish the prevailing pattern in lexicographic choices. Table 2 provides the data.

Table 2. Types of dictionary used by respondents

TYPES OF DICTIONARY	IN COLLEGE	FOR HOME STUDY
paper only	**15**	0
online only	0	**53**
electronic	0	0
combination of paper and online	**38**	0
none	0	0

Even a cursory look at the data in Table 2 reveals an overwhelming predominance and popularity of online dictionaries over the traditional printed ones. In the light of available research (see Section 2 of this chapter), these results are hardly surprising.

When asked to reflect on the reasons behind their use habits in question 2: *Have your dictionary use habits changed since you came to the English Studies department – why & why not?*, the respondents in their self-reports mostly confessed to a change in the use of the dictionary. Some of the answers they forwarded are presented in Table 3, grouped into four general headings.

Table 3. Reasons for changing habits of dictionary use

ACTION RECOMMENDED BY TEACHERS	BEFORE – TRANSLATION ONLY	NEW FUNCTIONS DISCOVERED	OTHER
"We need paper dictionaries for listening classes – the teacher insists"	"I used it to find the Polish or English translation of words"	"They have audio recordings of how to say words"	" I love my online one but I am ashamed to use it in class"
"I switched to a new online dictionary – diki – because the teacher showed me its functions"	"I needed the equivalents, I thought the definitions were too difficult"	"I like the examples and the idioms"	"I do not have the paper version at home, but I had to learn to use it here, it is too slow for me"
"The phonetics teacher demands correct phonetic script, so I need that and the audio"		"It shows links to other useful and related expressions"	"I was forbidden to use electronic devices in class"
		"It has phrases and sentences all recorded"	

The answers quoted above are representative of the ideas communicated by the respondents. Even if the exact wording was different, the ideas behind the words are similar. They are strongly indicative of two major trends: (1) that as dictionary users the respondents are rather adaptable to new demands and situations and (2) that they demonstrate a clear preference for online resources. Trend two was already conspicuous in answers to question 1, trend two may have certain pedagogical consequences, some of which will be discussed later on.

The next issue, partially embedded in the previous question, is whether their personal choices in terms of the specific dictionary they have used so far have changed as well. To clarify, they were not asked about which specific dictionary they used or are using now, the objective was to determine whether a selection or preference change has taken place – perhaps because of the reasons elaborated on previously and related to new use habits and needs. Question 3 (*Has your personal dictionary choice changed since you came to the English Studies department?*) was a multiple-choice one, with five possible answers which were constructed in such a way as to allow for a more in-depth interpretation of them.

Table 4. New or old dictionary

YES/NO	NUMBER OF RESPONSES	PERCENTAGES
Yes, I am using a new one	0	-
Yes, but I use a combination of old and new	31	58 %
Yes, because I didn't know of certain possibilities	18	33 %
No, I stick to the old favourite	0	-
No, I stick to the old one but use it differently	5	9 %

An interpretation of the data depicted in Table 4 allows us to make the following observation: with growing and changing needs of the subjects, they may need to revise their previous choices. They are willing to self-reflect and report on the most obvious motive for the change. Additionally, over a half of them admitted their option was to combine the old and the new, a trait that may disclose certain potential for opening them to new possibilities and resources.

Since our respondents exhibited a clear preference for online lexical resources, the next aim was to verify whether they are familiar with and/or actually use certain most widely known resources. It was worded in the following fashion: *Of the available online free dictionaries listed below, which one do you know of / have you used / do you currently use?* The subjects were asked to tick the relevant boxes and – if they wished so – to add a one-word comment on the frequency of use (occasionally, mostly, preferably, etc.). A sample answer, largely representative of the general result, is shown in Figure 1.

Figure 1. Sample answer as provided by a subject to question 4

4. *Of the available online free dictionaries listed below, which one do you ... ?*	*know of*	*have used*	*currently use*
translate google	✓		✓ (less)
diki.pl	✓		✓ (all the time)
Oxford Advanced online	✓		✓ (often)
Cambridge online	✓		
Collins Cobuild online			
merriam-webster.com	✓		
dictionary.reference.com			
thefreedicitonary.com			

Table 5 summarizes the answers given by all the 53 respondents. It transpires from the data obtained that while some available options are totally unknown to students, some others began to be used since the onset of their student careers. What must be seen as striking here is the overwhelming popularity of the Google Translate tool, frequently used indiscriminately without proper reflection on the lexical suggestions offered.

Table 5. Respondents' familiarity and use options of online dictionaries

OF THE AVAILABLE ONLINE FREE DICTIONARIES LISTED BELOW, WHICH ONE …?			
	DO YOU KNOW OF	HAVE YOU USED	DO YOU CURRENTLY USE
Google Translate	53	53	47
diki.pl	53	1	39
Oxford Advanced online	53	9	45
Cambridge online	35	-	22
Collins Cobuild online	-	-	-
merriam-webster.com	50	-	13
dictionary.reference.com	-	-	-
thefreedicitonary.com	-	-	-

In personal communication with randomly selected 12 respondents it turned out that the relative (un)familiarity with the available options underwent substantial modifications since they began their degree. Tutors kept suggesting their own preferred resources and explained why the one/s suggested are particularly relevant for the different purposes and different subjects. The most insistent of these suggestions came from teachers of pronunciation and oral/aural skills.

The subjects prove rather well acquainted with several online lexical resources and use them consciously. Therefore, they ought to be able to notice certain fundamentally classical features of a good, reliable and user-friendly online dictionary. Question 5 had the following form: *Which features do(es) the online dictionary/ies you use or know have/contain (tick all you recognize)?* and involved filling in a small table. Again, a sample is included in Figure 2 for clarification.

Figure 2. A sample of respondents' answers to question 5

Dictionary Name *Oxford OALD*	**Yes**	**No**	**Don't know**
Definition	✓		
Sample sentences	✓		
Collocations and related phrases			✓
IPA transcription	✓		
Audio pronunciation file	✓		
Audio files for the sample sentences and phrases		✓	

An analysis of answers provided by the students reveals that the *don't know* option was most frequently marked for features such as collocations (87 %) or audio files for sample sentences (51 %). The latter is not particularly surprising, bearing in mind that, to the best of the author's knowledge, only one online dictionary offers this particular application (*diki.pl*). And although this particular resource has been recommended to students many times, apparently most of them did not consider it important enough to take advantage of.

As a follow up to the previous question, the respondents were asked to create a personal ranking of the dictionary features from the previous task according to importance, understood here as usefulness for their immediate study needs. The most important criterion was placed highest, while the least important criterion was placed lowest. Figure 3 below depicts the mean ranking of six aspects connected with online dictionary use.

Figure 3. Mean ranking of selected dictionary features as expressed by respondents

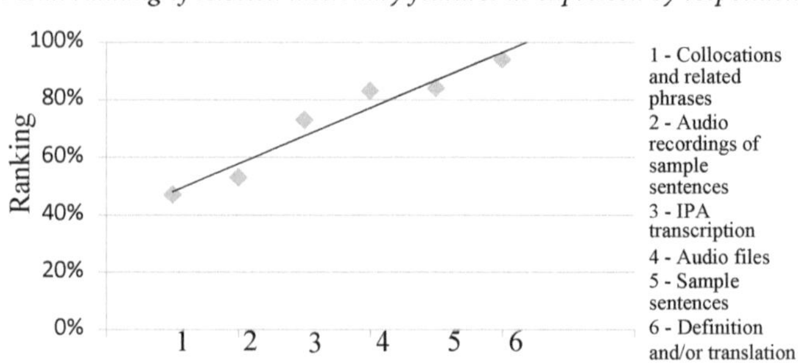

The results indicate that the individual ranking can be used as a reliable indicator of users' demands towards the online dictionary features and applications. The analysis of the ranking reveals that one aspect stands out above all the others and that is the item's definition and/or translation, which is hardly surprising when discussing learners' dictionary use. In addition to this, other, perhaps less classical, aspects in terms of traditional dictionaries but very characteristic of online ones, namely multimedia, were ranked rather high. Collocations and related phrases were ranked as (partly) unimportant, less relevant to students' needs than, for instance, the IPA transcription. The latter's position can be partially explained by the specificity of phonetic training in English Studies departments, where considerable attention is devoted to acquiring and frequent practicing of the transcription system.

In order to assess whether there are differences in the ranking dependable on other variables, a sub-group analysis was conducted. The variable selected was the participants' background – day or extramural students. It turned out that there are no dramatic ranking differences here, the first and last places in the ranking were identical. The different positions of other online dictionary features could be derived from the differences in the study needs of the participants and from the different sets of teachers with their own foci and expectations. The mean ranking as a function of different participants' background variable is shown in Figure 4 (for day) and Figure 5 (for extramurals), respectively.

Figure 4. Mean ranking of day students

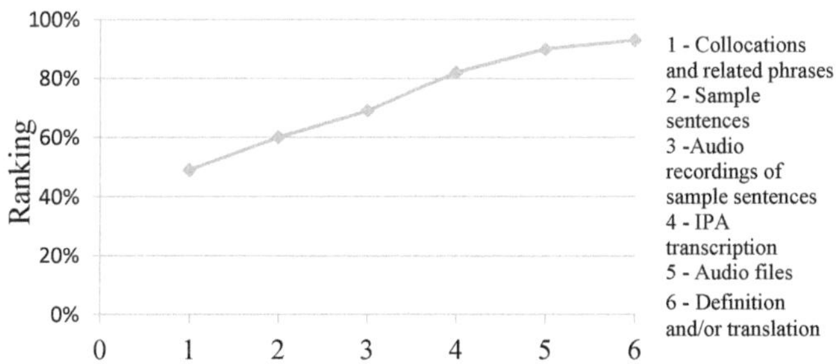

Figure 5. Mean ranking of extramural students

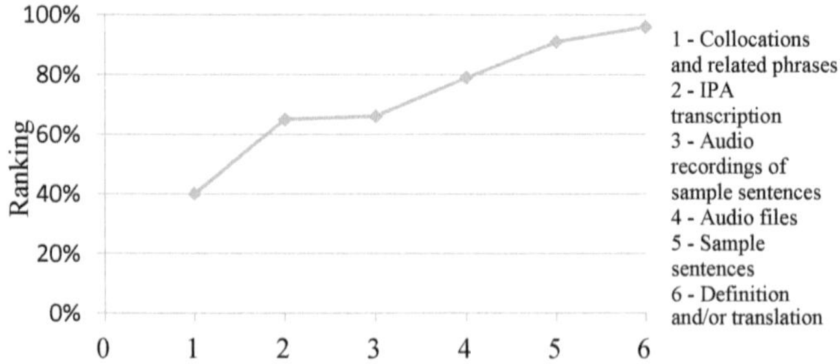

In relation to insights provided by the participants and personal communication with their lecturers an inquiry was made into the use of specific tools of the pronunciation apps (multimedia and IPA), available within the pronunciation section of a lexical item's entry, in relation to a specific context in which the development of English pronunciation skills takes place. The following question was asked: *You are always encouraged by your tutors to use the dictionaries to the full. In what way did they help you in developing your pronunciation?* Table 6 lists a selection of answers given by the respondents. They can be grouped into three major sub-categories: relating to the audio material, relating to the IPA transcription provided, and attention motives. The table presents but a fraction of the opinions reported, they can, however, be treated as representative of the views held by this particular group of respondents.

Table 6. Online dictionaries vs. developing pronunciation

RELATING TO AUDIO MATERIAL	RELATING TO IPA TRANSCRIPTION	ATTENTION MOTIVES
"I use them to help me with individual words"	"It is a great help for my phonetics homework"	"I rarely paid attention to them before, I do now"
"A teacher insists we always listen to them and repeat"	"I look at them and then listen to the audio and repeat them – a connection is made in this way"	"I realize now that I have to know exactly how to write words and how to say them"
"These are easier for me than IPA script"	"IPA is ok when it is impossible to play the audio"	"I check more words now before discussion classes, I don't want to make stupid mistakes"

RELATING TO AUDIO MATERIAL	RELATING TO IPA TRANSCRIPTION	ATTENTION MOTIVES
"I love the recordings of example sentences, I keep repeating them"	"I have to see the symbols to memorize them, being able to see them is helpful"	"I don't know how it was possible for me not to know and use IPA before!"
"By listening and repeating I am better prepared for my other English Skills Classes"		

For a small number of students it was very difficult to identify a specific area of influence, instead they wrote: "they help, I feel it but I don't know in which moments".

To improve the understanding of users' self-reports, they were asked to rate the usefulness of the pronunciation components (multimedia or otherwise) in the dictionary they use most often on a 5-point Likert scale, where 1 stands for "not really useful" and 5 - for "very useful indeed", all in relation to their personal needs and expectations. The features the respondents were asked to rate were: IPA transcription, audio pronunciation files, audio files accompanying the sample sentences and phrases, British and American variants and simulated spelling-based hints. Figure 6 shows the mean rating results, this time without any recourse to subgroup analysis, since such analysis did not produce any noteworthy differences.

Figure 6. Mean rating of pronunciation section of lexical entries

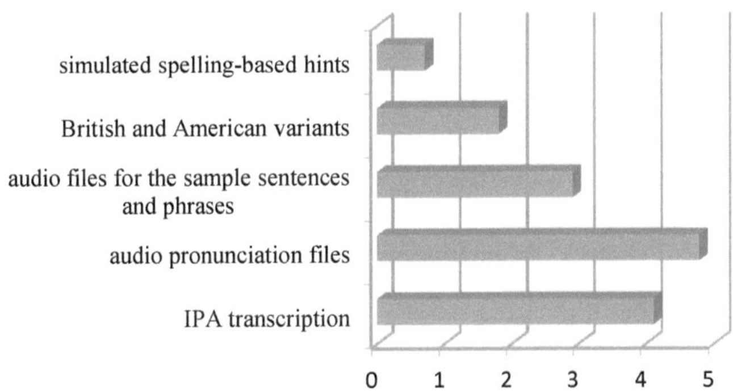

Combined with the answers obtained in the previous question, the ranking results confirm the participants' preference for multimedia help in improving their pronunciation.

The final question had the objective to evaluate the users' satisfaction with the online dictionary they use. The assumption was that if they have actually recommended a particular open online resource to their acquaintances, they consider it a useful, adaptable and relevant tool. The question was: *Have you recommended your current online dictionary to your friends or other people? Why?* A good proportion of students admitted they had done so, however, in several cases it seemed unnecessary, as the others either already knew of the resource and used it themselves or heard the same recommendation/insistence from their tutors. Among the many diverse reasons that prompted the recommendation, let us mention the ones particularly relevant to our interests here:

- more versatile and comprehensive resource, more than just definition/translation
- clear pronunciation information
- British pronunciation given first
- recordings not only of individual words but also whole sentence – good for connected speech practice
- excellent multimedia content
- nice voice in the audio files
- free accessibility

Opinions such as those listed above disclose a more and more conspicuous trend to pay attention to more than simply the meaning of new words or expressions. This in itself is a promising educational trend.

4.3. Discussion

The data from individual questions add up to build a more general picture of online dictionary use, at least in the group of respondents examined here.

The first observation is that the preference for online lexical resources is stable and growing. It confirms the ideas and trends observed earlier and reviewed in Section 2 of this chapter. What appears to be a new quality is the abandonment of the simplest, quickest tools, hitherto used indiscriminately to provide only the translation and/or meaning definition, in favour of more versatile and more comprehensive tools. It demonstrates that with their changing needs in terms of dictionary use, users become more reflective and more adaptable to new situations and challenges. They may still use, occasionally or not, the old tools for a quick check, but are prepared to complement that with resorting to resources recommended to them as students of English Studies departments.

That such recommendations are made and are accepted has become obvious from the data obtained. As a result, the ways the students use online dictionaries now have been modified in comparison to their earlier practices. One example is the changed consultation practice because of the growing emphasis on students producing a nice flow of good quality English.

The recommendations do not flow only from the tutors to the students, as the latter begin to share their experiences with other students. As a result, an expanding network of new dictionary use practices develops and more knowledge sharing takes place. For that to happen, a certain degree of insistence on familiarizing themselves with new resource options and the functions/ features therein is needed. Therefore, a demand is created for more rational dictionary consultation training, pinpointing the various functions and encouraging a more innovative and open-minded approach to what an online dictionary can offer.

It appears that the effort invested in training participants to use the lexical resources holistically enables both better personalization of instruction and actual improvement in one of the educational areas. It follows the idea to openly innovate in teaching and learning. The opinions ventured by the respondents testify to a more aware utilization of available resources, coupled with improved findability and usability of the required and needs-relevant elements.

The participants, alongside the need to expand their lexical stock, currently also understand and embrace the necessity of developing better pronunciation skills, as these are perceived essential in successful communication. This makes them more aware dictionary users and more open to appreciate the new possibilities included in the online resources that they make use of. Although it has not been attempted in the present study, a re-evaluation of the rating and ranking of several good online dictionary features (Müller-Spitzer and Koplenig 2014; see Section 2 of this chapter) may produce different results. The users have now learned to use online resources in more comprehensive ways, paying attention to features that online, but not paper, dictionaries can easily provide.

In a small-scale research such as the one carried out for the purposes of this chapter, it is impossible to tackle the very many aspects of dictionary use that there are. The focus was on the potential assistance online dictionaries can provide when it comes to developing students' oral skills. The investigations still demonstrate the need for training students in taking advantage of the possibilities offered to the full. The fact that the respondents combine and complement the available resources testifies to their dissatisfaction with suboptimal solutions – a tendency most welcome for any educator. Locating a pronunciation-assisting feature in a dictionary may actually determine how useful or helpful the dictionary is in a specific educational context.

5. Conclusions

If learning is dependent upon attention and the quality of information processing, then effective teaching should include training which directs the learner's attention to the complete form of the words targeted for instruction and require students to innovatively apply the available open and free resources. It is the hope of many instructors that with the growing findability of certain features in online lexical resources, usability will grow. This, in turn, can be contrasted with user-friendliness – as transpires from the data obtained, the mere existence of a particular multimedia feature or other pronunciation information does not immediately guarantee its use. It can only happen if the potential user feels it is maximally tailored to their specific needs – in our case the needs were those of advanced EFL speakers who wished and, at the same time, were required to develop and improve their oral performance in English.

It is clear to the wide public that the Web is with us to stay. One striking development of the recent decades has been an explosion of online-based dictionaries. These are willingly and enthusiastically used by advanced EFL speakers in ways they had not thought of before. The interaction between the online tool and the user has become different in the researched group. Even in their self-reflections they see that with the growing competence in English, they become more open to ideas that underline the meaningfulness of attention paid equally to the form of words as well as the meaning. As a result, they are prepared to modify their choices and habits of dictionary use to meet those newly-arisen needs. If fact, the students quickly realised that their old favourites - most notably *Google Translate* - were no longer sufficient, or even satisfactory. Therefore, they opted for combinations of resources that would guarantee a reasonable degree of usefulness, online helping tools and contribution to incidental (vocabulary and pronunciation) learning. This could arguably be seen as a contribution to a more open education.

References

Atkins, Beryl T. Sue (ed.)
1998 *Using Dictionaries. Studies of Dictionary Use by Language Learners and Translators*. Tübingen: Max Niemeyer Verlag.

Dashtestani, Reza
2013 "EFL teachers' and students' perspectives on the use of electronic dictionaries for learning English", *Computer-Assisted Language Learning – Electronic Journal*, *14*(2), 51–65.

Duke, Betsy - Ginger Harper - Mark Johnston
2013 "Connectivism as a digital age learning theory". *The International HETL Review. Special Issue*, 4–13.

Hulstijn, Jan H. - Beryl T. Sue Atkins
1998 "Empirical research on dictionary use in foreign-language learning: Survey and discussion", in Beryl T. Sue Atking (ed.), 7–19.

Koplenig, Alexander - Carolin Müller-Spitzer
2014 "General issues of online dictionary use", in Carolin Müller-Spitzer (ed.), 127–141.

Lew, Robert
2014 "Opportunities and limitations of user studies", in Carole Tiberius - Carolin Müller-Spitzer (eds.), 5–15.

Müller-Spitzer, Carolin - Alexander Koplenig
2014 "Online dictionaries: expectations and demands", in: Carolin Müller-Spitzer (ed.), 143–188.

Müller-Spitzer, Carolin (ed.)
2014 *Using Online Dictionaries*. Berlin, Boston: De Gruyter.

Oblinger, Diana G. (ed.)
2012 *Game changers: Education and Information Technologies*, Educause. Available at: http://www.educause.edu/research-publications/books/game-changers-education-and-information-technologies (date of access: 8 March 2016).

Peter, Sandra - Markus Deimann
2013 "On the role of openness in education: A historical reconstruction.", *Open Praxis*, *5*(1), 7–14.

Siemens, George
2004 "Connectivism: A Learning Theory for the Digital Age". Available at: http://www.elearnspace.org/Articles/connectivism.htm (date of access: 9 March 2016).

Tarp, Sven
2014 "Detecting user needs for new online dictionary projects", in Carole Tiberius - Carolin Müller-Spitzer (eds.), 16–26.

Tiberius, Carole - Carolin Müller-Spitzer (eds.)
2014 *Research into dictionary use* Wörterbuchbenutzungsforschung. 5. Arbeitsbericht des wissenschaftlichen Netzwerks „Internetlexikografie". – Mannheim: Institut für Deutsche Sprache. (erscheint in: OPAL – Online publizierte Arbeiten zur Linguistik 2015), preprint version, Available at: http://ids-pub.bsz-bw.de/solrsearch/index/search/searchtype/series/id/11/rows/10 (date of access: 8 March 2016).

Tono, Yukio
2001 *Research on Dictionary Use in the Context of Foreign Language Learning.* Tübingen: Max Niemeyer Verlag.

Wiley, David
2016 'The Consensus Around "Open"'. Available at: http://opencontent.org/blog/page/3 (date of access: 8 March 2016).

Wiley, David - Cable Green
2012 " Why openness in education?", in Diana G. Oblinger (ed.), 81–89.

Anna Turula
Pedagogical University, Kraków, Poland

University Education in the Digital Age – Are We Open?

Abstract
This chapter looks at the use of new technologies in academic education, with special regard to a TEFL training programme. An insight is offered into the process of hybrid tutoring of a group of students writing their MA theses on new technologies in language education. The chapter presents the results of a study carried out, in an action-research-mode, alongside the tutoring process. The data come from three different sources: a student satisfaction survey; the quantitative and qualitative analysis of the discourse of the tutorials, both face-to-face and in-cloud; as well as the observation journal kept by the tutor. As the student satisfaction and discourse studies are described in more detail in two other publications (Turula 2014; Turula in press), the present chapter will describe these two briefly, concentrating on the teacher's perspective. It will be argued here that – when employing new technologies in academic education – the teacher needs to keep an open mind in many different ways.

Keywords: university education, blended learning, tutorial, cloud computing, Pygmalion effect

1. Introduction

Reflecting on education at a certain moment in time has to revolve around two important issues. First of all, it is necessary to remember what is timeless and, therefore, worth adhering to. Secondly – and equally importantly – attention should be paid to what makes education modern and what contemporary trends are worth pursuing. This refers to education in general as well as to different individual areas of schooling, including language learning and – more specifically – university education, which is the focus of the present chapter.

Considering both issues, the timeless and the modern in education, one needs to keep on open mind, being sensitive to a number of problems. The timeless is often called the traditional and given up for the sake of the modern, which may not always be the desired course of action. On the other hand, the question of keeping up with the modern is eagerly answered with new technologies. Obvious as it is 16 years into the new millennium, this tendency can actually foster the undesirable old ways if all that is modern about education is the mere use of digital tools.

This chapter looks at both sides of the coin, aiming to propose a balanced approach in which the modern and the timeless are successfully merged. In doing so, it starts by pinpointing potential mindtraps of thinking about education in time. Then it shows some pedagogical solutions, their outcomes – especially for the teacher herself – and implications. These solutions have been devised for an MA seminar in TEFL. Yet, the philosophy behind course design pertains, hopefully, to other areas of education.

1. Delineating the context

1.1 The trap of the modern

When considering education with a certain willingness to be open to new solutions, it is easy to fall into a number of mindtraps. One of such pitfalls is an either-or approach, based on viewing schooling through dichotomies such as *now* vs. *then*, *modern* vs. *traditional*, etc. Another way of putting on pedagogical shutters is to always follow the latest trends and discard the old ways without a moment's thought; or, on the contrary, to adhere to the old mindset, immune to change, regardless of potential benefits. The mindtraps are given a thorough look below, in the hope that a better understanding may help us brace ourselves against them.

1.1.1 Limited by dichotomies

Innovation in language teaching and the resulting encouragement for openness to the novel trends are frequently introduced in opposition to current practice. In doing so, the proponents of the new frequently juxtapose its elements with relevant aspects of the old model. An example of such a one-to-one comparison is presented in Figure 1.

Figure 1. Educational dichotomies: ins and outs (CC-NC-ND by Gerstein 2014)

Education Ins	Education Outs
Learner as the center of instruction	Content as the center of instruction
Educator as a coach, mentor, guide, resource, and lead learner	Teacher as the expert and deliverer of content, tests, assignments, discipline
Use of the internet to get a pluralistic, broad perspective of a topic	Use of a single textbook to teach a subject
Failure and mistakes are seen as part of the learning process.	Perfection is explicitly and implicitly expected by and for both students and teachers.
Differentiated and personalized curriculum	One-size-fits-all curriculum
Ongoing, formative assessments for and by students to increase learning	Summative assessments for accountability of teachers and the school
Learning is multi-sensory, hands-on, authentic, and relevant	Learning is typically only focused with only with the brain in mind, sometimes not seen as relevant by the students
Learners produce as well as consume content	Students spend most of their time consuming content created by others
Learners doing more talking and working than the educator during class time	Teachers do most of the work and talking during class time
Technology seamlessly integrated into the curriculum	Technology as an add-on, specialty, or afterthought.
Misbehavior is viewed as an opportunity for growth & often resolved through group effort	Misbehavior is disciplined by the teacher
Social emotional learning seen as an integral to educating the whole child	Social emotional learning minimally or not integrated into learning

Such juxtapositions are very appealing; they look neat and elegant, and, as such, satisfy our need for order, logic and predictability of the world around us. In doing so, however, they also offer processing ease which lulls our mind to sleep – instead of opening it – and makes us forget that the world happens to be more complicated and, consequently, more interesting. And thinking along the lines of either-or, we can lose sight of the bigger picture.

First of all, while it is rather unquestionable that "learning should be multi-sensory, hands-on, authentic and relevant", and not "only focused with the brain in mind", categorising other statements as desirable (ins) or undesirable (outs) (Figure 1) is intellectually limiting. The fact that "misbehaviour is viewed as an opportunity for growth" does not rule out the fact that it should be disciplined. Similarly, formative evaluation need not exclude summative assessment, especially that the latter serves an important documentation function in the educational world in which course completion is still frequently based on the final outcome. This is closely linked to a one-size-fits-all curriculum, which in this context seems to be mandatory rather than simply passé. There can be no doubt that it should be differentiated and personalised, but rather in *how* it is introduced, and not so much as to *what* is taught. Yet, a conclusion that we should replace alternatives with conjunctions is equally misleading because the appropriate balancing of the two sides of the coin is always a function of context: it is the teacher who needs to decide what is – in a given situation – of more value: disciplining the troublemaker or using the incident for pedagogical reasons; offering descriptive or sum-up feedback; individualising or setting universal standards and requirements.

A similar need for contextualisation occurs in the case of a number of other ins and outs. This is because questions in education are rarely close-ended and the answer very frequently should start with *It depends.* Whether the Internet is better than a textbook depends on the quality of the latter as well as on how well the students can avoid the effect of the filter bubble (Pariser 2011) if the course-book text is replaced by the online content. The phenomenon, introduced and explained by Pariser, excludes, rather than promotes, the broadness and plurality of perspectives while a well-written textbook can be very effective in this area. The (un)desirability of other descriptors (see Figure 1) may also depend on individual differences regarding both the teacher and the learner. Some students prefer consuming content to creating it; they are also more comfortable with expert-teachers than with teacher-facilitators (Turula 2011); and expectations of perfection are only natural in achievement-oriented learners. In turn, using technology, a *signum temporis* as it is, may not agree with some teaching styles or the specificity of some classes (Physical Education?). Besides, even if dedicated to seamlessly integrating the new media into the teaching process, the teacher may – occasionally – opt for the add-on mode, especially in a syllabus-flexible blended class in which new technologies are used reactively, in response to individual learning problems.

All in all, as most experienced educators are likely to agree, good education is of the *between* quality: balanced, reflective, trying to account for different aspects of the learning context. While dichotomies may have the advantage of helping us categorise reality, they can also be detrimental to how open-minded we are about this reality in general and our pedagogy in particular.

1.1.2 Blinded by new technologies

When adopting a temporal perspective on education, our vantage point is usually the present with its trends that are likely to affect school. In examining such trends in the year 2016, the spotlight is usually on new technologies, which have become a constant in our lives. An example of such a spotlight is the *NMC Horizon Report*[1],

1 The report is compiled annually by two non-profit organisations: the international New Media Consortium and the EDUCAUSE Learning Initiative, an association for the promotion of new media in the academia. The report, which is recognised worldwide, is the work of renowned new technologies' experts and practitioners from all over the globe (the 2015 Report was prepared by 52 persons from 16 countries on 6 continents).

which prognosticates how modern media are going to influence the way we learn and teach. The outlook for 2015–2020[2] is presented in Figure 2.

What most theoreticians point out (in Poland, Morbitzer 2009 and 2010) – and what practitioners claim to adhere to – is that these trends need to be seen in a broader pedagogical context. In other words, the inspiration that comes from publications such as the report cannot boil down to simple linear recommendations like:

> **If Horizon experts prognosticate an increased popularity of social media in education (Figure 2), it is necessary to extend learning spaces into the most popular social networking sites (SNSs)**.

What is needed is – again – an open mind and a deeper kind of reflection. Following the nodes presented in Figure 3 and answering the questions posed in them we are likely to realise that social media stand for networking (including knowledge connectivity), socialising, co-creation of content, verbality and non-verbality in interactions as well as (immediate) feedback, flattening of hierarchies, etc. Only with these aspects identified can we confront what social media stand for with our own teaching philosophy and decide if all the different facets fit into it; or – if they do not – resolve how keen we are on modifying our approach to teaching.

Figure 2. NMC Horizon Report (2015: 35); CC-BY 3.0

Consumer Technologies
> 3D Video
> Drones
> Electronic Publishing
> Mobile Apps
> Quantified Self
> Tablet Computing
> Telepresence
> Wearable Technology

Digital Strategies
> Bring Your Own Device (BYOD)
> Flipped Classroom
> Games and Gamification
> Location Intelligence
> Makerspaces
> Preservation/Conservation Technologies

Internet Technologies
> Cloud Computing
> The Internet of Things
> Real-Time Translation
> Semantic Applications
> Single Sign-On
> Syndication Tools

Learning Technologies
> Badges/Microcredit
> Learning Analytics
> Massive Open Online Courses
> Mobile Learning
> Online Learning
> Open Content
> Open Licensing
> Virtual and Remote Laboratories

Social Media Technologies
> Collaborative Environments
> Collective Intelligence
> Crowdfunding
> Crowdsourcing
> Digital Identity
> Social Networks
> Tacit Intelligence

Visualization Technologies
> 3D Printing/Rapid Prototyping
> Augmented Reality
> Information Visualization
> Visual Data Analysis
> Volumetric and Holographic Displays

Enabling Technologies
> Affective Computing
> Cellular Networks
> Electrovibration
> Flexible Displays
> Geolocation
> Location-Based Services
> Machine Learning
> Mesh Networks
> Mobile Broadband
> Natural User Interfaces
> Near Field Communication
> Next-Generation Batteries
> Open Hardware
> Speech-to-Speech Translation
> Statistical Machine Translation
> Virtual Assistants
> Wireless Power

2 The 2016 report to be released in Feb 2016.

Figure 3. A pedagogy-motivated approach to new technological trends

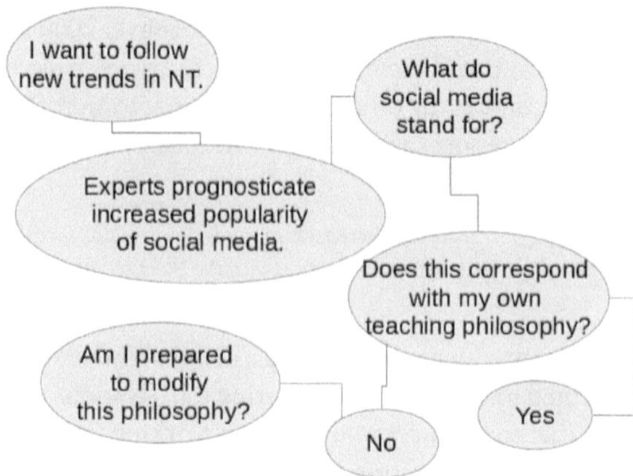

In practice, however, the linear recommendations and the following (not fully successful – see Lantz-Andersson et al. 2013) educational applications of the new media seem to be undesirably frequent. This is probably the result of a certain ICT-blindness that affects some teachers who decide to use the new media in their classroom. This blindness is caused by the assumption that mere digitalisation of teaching can significantly improve the quality of the instruction offered. This attitude transpires from a number of recent reports on distance education in Poland[3] as well as from the practice of academic e-learning in our country. The reports show considerable satisfaction of teachers and decision makers implementing elements of online learning in their schools, which looks unfounded if seen in the context of what new technologies are customarily used for in Polish schools: making handouts available and exchanging email with students (based on the same reports). When it comes to the academia, a considerable pressure put on teachers to facilitate classes both off- and online is rarely followed by: authentic quality control aimed at the evaluation of e-content and e-course design; CAL[4]-oriented staff training; and admin support. Instead, popular practices involve: evaluation

3 Chomczyński et al. *Diagnoza stanu kształcenia na odległość w Polsce i wybranych krajach Unii Europejskiej oraz potrzeb edukacyjnych polskich nauczycieli i odbiorców w zakresie kształcenia na odległość* and *Sprawozdanie z realizacji Rządowego programu rozwijania kompetencji uczniów i nauczycieli w zakresie stosowania technologii informacyjno – komunikacyjnych „Cyfrowa szkoła"*. 2014.

4 Computer Assisted Learning

criteria such as *Are there crosswords in the e-course?*; or training sessions limited to purely technical instruction, if any are offered at all.

The foregrounding of technology *per se* may be the legacy of a certain T-shirt caption: *If you can't beat them, join them*, once popularly used to advertise e-learning. The caption aimed at pointing out to teachers that their students – digital natives, as Prensky (2001) called them – can only be truly educated in their natural habitat, which is online. 15 years after the publication we already know that the digital native is overrated and we, digital immigrants, have a lot to teach him/her on different levels of digital literacy, with special regard to: competences related to search and evaluation of online content; attentive monotasking; understanding discourse other than MMO-speak; the educational side of the Internet; and many others. In spite of this, though, teachers seem stuck in the *join-them* mode, hoping that a bit of the computer *alone* is going to make a substantial change in schooling. This, however, is a dangerous illusion. First of all, as it was stated above, digital natives already know computers; what they need are the competences beyond. As a result, to make education modern one needs new literacies and a new attitude rather than just new technologies. Otherwise, as shown in the two Polish reports cited above, blinded by the digital, teachers may not realise that ICT is actually a cover-up for pedagogy which is traditional in the most pejorative sense of the word: transmissive and teacher-centred.

The new attitude sanctioning education that would be truly up-to-date should be based on extensive reflection (see Figure 3), as a result of which new technologies could be used not just to regale the so-called digital native but, primarily, on condition that: (i) online instruction is actually more effective than a similar offline routine; (ii) digital tools are affordanced properly – in terms of task-tool as well as learner-tool matching – and used with a purpose, and not just for the art's sake; and (iii) the pedagogy is *digital* not only, and not primarily, when it capitalises on and reinforces technological literacy; it is *digital* in the sense that it assists an individual learner and fosters teacher freedom, promotes individualised as well as collaborative learning, and leads to the flattening of hierarchies for the sake of genuine dialogue and sincere feedback. In other words, *the computer*, for which the C in CAL stands, needs to be understood metonymically: as the machine itself (in its currently most popular form – PC, laptop, tablet, mobile phone) and – more importantly – through all the applications it is currently put to by its users.

2. Balanced between the modern and the timeless

2.1 The study

An attempt at implementing a pedagogical solution following the framework delineated in section 1 – *digital* in the sense defined towards the end of Section 1.1.2; based on thorough reflection recommended in the conclusion to Section 1.1.1 – was made in an MA seminar taught at the School of English of the Pedagogical University in Kraków in the spring term of 2014.

The class was taught in a hybrid mode, as a series of off- and online tutorials. The offline meetings lasted 30 minutes, and each of them was devoted to essay reading (15 mins) and the following discussion, in which the tutor asked questions concerning the essay and the tutee answered them (15 mins). The online meetings were unrestricted in time, but for the two-week time frame within which the student and the teacher worked on one essay. They were carried out on Google Drive, in which the student made the essay available to the tutor, who asked questions using the *comment* function. These questions were answered by the tutee, with the ask-answer process being usually repeated, or – occasionally – in real time via Google Drive chat.

The participants of the class were 9 first-year students of the TEFL MA programme at the Pedagogical University in Kraków, Poland. Each of the students took part in 4 tutorials scheduled at two-week intervals, 2 face-to-face meetings and 2 digital classes via Google Drive.

The design of the class was motivated by the teacher's interactive and dialogic educational philosophy. First and foremost, this philosophy underlay the choice of the tutorial method, which is based on one-to-one meetings between the teacher and the student, devoted to essay reading and discussion. What was particularly important was that every such meeting was individualized, based on the knowledge the tutor had gained about the student, and student-centred as the tutor always shifted the focus onto the student, by asking eye-opening questions rather than lecturing. The teacher's preferred approach also led to the selection of the digital tool used in the online part of the blended class. Required were the following functions of the tool: (i) the possibility for the student to share a body of text with the tutor; (ii) the possibility for the teacher and the student to comment on this text and respond to comments, synchronously and asynchronously; (iii) the availability of the tool to all the parties involved. Based on these criteria, Google Drive was used as the medium. In this sense, digitalisation was the consequence of pedagogy, and not the main focus of it. Yet, when used, it not only subserved but also reinforced the teaching mode, adding to its dialogic nature, open-endedness and individualisation. It was also the blended format resulting from the balance between the traditional (tutoring) and the modern (cloud computing) that improved the effectiveness of the tutorials.

2.2 Student satisfaction and learning

The claims above agree with the results of the student satisfaction survey carried out at the end of the course (see also Turula 2014). The survey was filled in by all the nine participants of the course. The general contentment with the class was rated quite high (5.33 on a scale of 1–6). As for the comments regarding the strong and weak points of each mode of the tutor-tutee interaction, the students generally paid attention to: the dialectic character of the education offered; the individualisation of instruction and (lack of) direct teacher-student contact; as well as the anytime/anywhere mode of the online part of the course. The possibility to dialogue with the teacher on a one-to-one basis (9 out of 9 respondents) and the question-not-lecture mode (7/9) are listed as the strong points of both traditional and CMC meetings. At the same time, the students ascribe different – and mutually complementing – advantages to the two tuition modes. All students (9/9) value face-to-face meetings over the online encounters for the direct contact with the tutor. At the same time, however, they admit that the digital tutorials had a definite virtue of enabling the dialogue to happen in what one student referred to as *slow motion*: the lack of time constraints resulted, according to the students surveyed, in a much deeper level of processing in the tutor-tutee exchanges. Most students (7/9) valued the online format for the time to think before answering the tutor's questions which, as all of them admit, helped them better prepare for the ultimate goal of the class – writing and defending their MA thesis.

The fact that the face-to-face mode had a positive effect on motivation and interpersonal dynamics while the online tutorials promoted critical thinking is proved by the analysis of the discourse of the tutorials. As the study was described in detail in another publication (Turula, in press), the present chapter will report the main finding only. The discourse of the face-to-face and online tutorials, analysed for 6 out of the 9 participants[5], shows that when considered vis à vis the four categories of cognitive presence (Garrison et al. 2001), for all six students the number of resolutions ([RES] – the highest category on a scale of critical thinking) in CMC is considerably higher than in traditional tutoring, in spite of the much less intense cognitive presence of the other three kinds: [TRIG], [EXP] and [INT].

5 For the remaining 3 students the records were incomplete, for example one recording / one online essay comments were missing.

This may suggest that the effort spent on triggering, exploration and integration, both off- and online, is inversely proportional to the outcome of these intellectual endeavours; in other words, online better outcomes are achieved faster (for a more detailed analysis see Turula, in press). In turn, as regards social presence (Rourke et al. 2001), it is much more intense in the traditional meeting if evaluated on the basis of the numbers of individual responses. However, the f2f /e differences for affective and – especially – interactive responses in favour of traditional tutoring are much more significant than in the case of triggers, explorations or integration (for a more detailed analysis see Turula, in press).

What transpires from the results is the mutually compensatory character of the two modes: the face-to-face and the online. The former had all the advantages of direct teacher-student contact: immediate feedback, verbal and non-verbal, the motivating atmosphere, and what the students saw as the personal touch. However, the offline tutorials were time-constrained, with all the consequences of this. Cloud tutorials, in turn, even though devoid of the immediate contact, posed no limits on either participant of the process, giving both the student and the teacher ample time to reflect on their contributions to the dialogue. For the student, it resulted in the activation of higher-order thinking: more profound analysis; attempts at model building; resolution; and reference to literature.

2.3 What the teacher learned

In addition to the advantages of the blended mode described above, and based on the teacher journal, two aspects of the online pedagogy need to be discussed separately; and from the teacher's rather than the student's perspective. The in-cloud mode – much more than the traditional mode – equipped the tutor with a powerful educational tool: asking questions (typical of tutoring) which were especially carefully considered (cloud tutoring does not happen in real time) in terms of both the content and the form. As a result, the questions asked online did not only trigger deep student thinking; they were also tactful and showed the tutor's belief that at the other end of the Internet connection there was a reflective human being, capable of addressing the teacher's enquiries in an intelligent way. Owing to the consideration, the tact and the belief, the answers offered were usually up to the tutor's standards: the students became good students because they were seen as such by the tutor. This is known as the Pygmalion effect (Rosenthal and Jacobson 1968) and could indeed be frequently observed in teacher/student exchanges (based on the teacher journal).

All this leads to an interesting observation; and a slightly unorthodox one. Most pedagogical innovation is introduced for the sake of the student with his/

her best interest in mind. The blended tutoring described here resulted in a number of such benefits to the tutees, cognitive (higher-order thinking) and affective (increased motivation), as described in Section 2.2. Yet, what appears equally interesting is how the balancing between the face-to-face and the digital benefited the teacher; and that the Pygmalion effect seems to have worked on the teacher equally powerfully.

First of all, the language of teacher feedback acquired new quality. As shown in samples 1–4 (all of which are authentic excerpts from student-teacher exchanges in cloud tutorials), the abrupt ways of evaluation popularly used by teachers – and, admittedly, by the tutor described herself – gave way to more tactful modes of expression. The old *It's unclear*, *off-topic*, *incoherent* and *incorrect* were replaced by requests for clarification, refining/focussing and awareness raising (see Samples 1–4).

Sample 1. Two excerpts from a teacher (T)/student (S) cloud dialogue
'It's unclear' *anew*

(a)
T (about matching quiz difficulty to learner IDs): What do you mean, exactly?
S: There are also differences among listenings on the same proficiency level. Each speaker has characteristic pace, pitch etc. which may be incomprehensible (=too difficult) for particular student.
T: Now I get it, thx

(b)
T: I must confess I don't really get the point you are making here …
S: Students also evaluate the materials in some way. When they find them boring or useless they will not feel eager to use them what may result in some discipline problems and negative attitude to the teacher.
T: OK.

Sample 2. Two excerpts from a teacher (T)/student (S) cloud dialogue
'It's off-topic' *anew*

(a)
T: To which of the two school systems does this relate and how?
S: In the context of my essay it relates to Montessori schools, however, in a wider context it really refers to both schools as they learn and encourage children to develop empathy.

(b)
T: How can all this be related to new technologies?
S: New technology devices give us opportunity to receive and send information to people from all over the world. In order to rise students' intercultural awareness, teachers can organize projects which would include video conferences with students from a different country. What is more, if some students are especially

interested in a particular culture they can use the Internet to find different materials: photos, articles and videos. They don't have to go a distant country (which can be really expensive) if they want to learn something about this particular culture.
T: That is certainly pertinent to intercultural skills, thank you. How about the development of social and emotional skills?

Sample 3. Two excerpt from a teacher (T)/student (S) cloud dialogue
'It's incoherent' *anew*

(a)
T: Is this related somehow to the previous paragraph? If yes, how?
S: It is partly related to the previous paragraph in the way that it tells about teacher's role in the classroom and his attitude towards students. The previous paragraph also focuses on one of the teacher's roles which is the role of an assessor. As an assessor, the teacher does two things, that is, correcting and organizing feedback.

(b)
T (about meaningful feedback): In what way is this related to "meaning" as defined above, in relation to the PERMA model?
S: Student's work in both approaches needs to be meaningful. In competency-based learning a teacher shows the meaning of student's work by using feedback
T: And more specifically? (this, only if you have already defined meaning, and broadly :-))

Sample 4. Two excerpts from a teacher (T)/student (S) cloud dialogue
'It's incorrect' *anew*

(a)
T: Could you clarify the meaning of this phrase, pls?
S: I have rechecked this phrase and it does not really reflect what I meant. What I should have written instead is that "The grading system of gamification works in student's favour…"
T: Thank you

(b)
T: Why would you use "evolve" and not "change", "developed" or other verbs? Is there a reason?
S: The use of the verb 'evolve ' was intentional. I wanted to emphasize the fact that methods and techniques in teaching children developed gradually, together with various spheres of human life. I wanted to show that it was a process and not an instant change or progress.
T: OK :-)

What needs to be emphasised is that while some of the exchanges are eye-opening for the student (S) – Sample 4a – most result in the tutee standing his/her ground (also in terms of the form used – Sample 4b); refining their argument (1a); steering towards the main focus (2 a and 2b); or improving coherence (3a and b). As a result, in all the cases the technique, owing to its open-endedness, is face-saving for the student: even if in the wrong, s/he can reason his/her way out of the content and stylistic pitfalls. Yet, equally importantly, by avoiding the abruptness of the customarily used comments, the teacher is also able to avoid the threat to her own face posed by any kind of confrontation one chooses to get into.

What is important to point out is that the changes are not purely stylistic. The real Pygmalion effect in the teacher's case is a permanent improvement of attitude to students. Behaving tactfully, empathetically and with the focus on the good in the student, the teacher herself becomes more tactful, empathetic and trusting in principle. This is illustrated by an authentic email to a student who failed to keep an important deadline. Sample 5 shows its original, abrupt wording as well as the final version that resulted from the careful consideration of the potential cause of the delay and, consequently, the wording of the message.

Sample 5. An email that evolved

Dear XYZ, *I'm very sorry to say this but if You do not participate, you will not get course credit.* *Yours* *Teacher*	→	*Dear XYZ,* *I've known you as a reliable person. Now I see you do not participate. Is anything the matter? Are you OK?* *Yours (concerned)* *Teacher*

Conclusions

The pedagogy used in the MA seminar was based on the approach that balanced the timeless (tutoring; the question mode that can be traced back as far as Socratic teaching; the Pygmalion effect) with the up-to-date (cloud computing, included in the master list of tracked technologies to influence education). The combination, as hopefully proved in the course designing process described in the present chapter, was based on reflection, as a result of which a combination of techniques – rather than the either-or alternative – was adopted. This, with regard to the benefits to the students and the teacher herself, seems to be a worthwhile example of university education at the onset of the 21st century. As emphasised throughout the chapter, such education requires an open mind and reflection. The results of such openness for both the student and the teacher, quite unsurprisingly, are an open mind and reflection. The case of the educator seems particularly noteworthy here as it demonstrates that openness in education is not simply a question of paradigm change; it is also – and more importantly – about the preparedness for constant change, an ongoing readiness to accept what we learn while educating others and to adjust our ways, accordingly.

References

Chomczyński, Piotr – Ewa Głowacka – Dominik Mytkowski – Michał Naftyński – Ewa Niedzielska – Wojciech Zieliński

2013 *Diagnoza stanu kształcenia na odległość w Polsce i wybranych krajach Unii Europejskiej oraz potrzeb edukacyjnych polskich nauczycieli i odbiorców w zakresie kształcenia na odległość.*_Available at: https://depot.ceon.pl/handle/123456789/2988 (date of access 20 January 2016).

Garrison, D. Randy – Terry Anderson – Walter Archer

2001 "Critical thinking, cognitive presence, and computer conferencing in distance education", *American Journal of Distance Education, 15*(1), 7–23.

Gerstein, Jackie

2014 What's in and what's out in education. *User Generated Education.* https://usergeneratededucation.wordpress.com/2014/01/10/whats-in-and-whats-out-in-education (date of access: 20 January 2016).

Lantz-Andersson, Annika – Sylvi Vigmo – Rhonwen Bowen

2013 "Crossing boundaries in Facebook: Students' framing of language learning activities as extended spaces", *International Journal of Computer-Supported Collaborative Learning, 8*(3), 293–312.

Morbitzer, Janusz

2009 "Interakcja człowiek – Internet – refleksje pedagogiczne", in Janusz Morbitzer (ed.), 177–183.

2010 "Szkoła w pułapce Internetu", in J. Morbitzer (ed.), 18–27.

NMC Horizon Report

2015 Available at: http://cdn.nmc.org/media/2015-nmc-horizon-report-HE-EN.pdf (date of access: 20 January 2016).

Pariser, Eli

2011 *The Filter Bubble: How the New Personalized Web Is Changing What We Read and How We Think.* London: Penguin.

Prensky, Michael
2001 "Digital natives, digital immigrants". Available at: http://www.marcprensky.com/writing/Prensky%20-%20Digital%20Natives,%20Digital%20Immigrants%20-%20Part1.pdf (date of access: 20 January 2016).

Rosenthal, Robert – Lenore Jacobson
1968 *Pygmalion in the Classroom*. New York: Holt, Rinehart & Winston.

Rourke, Liam – Terry Anderson – D. Randy Garrison – Walter Archer
2001 "Assessing social presence in asynchronous text-based computer conferencing", *Journal of Distance Education, 14*(2).

Sprawozdanie z realizacji Rządowego programu rozwijania kompetencji uczniów i nauczycieli w zakresie stosowania technologii informacyjno – komunikacyjnych „Cyfrowa szkoła"
2014 Available at: http://www.kuratorium.gda.pl/pliki/SPRAWOZDANIECYFROWASZKOLA-przyjeteprzezRM25_02_2014-1.pdf (date of access: 20 January 2016).

Turula, Anna
2011 *Form-Focused Instruction and the Advanced Language Learner. On the Importance of the Semantics of Grammar.* Frankfurt: Peter Lang.
2014 "Kiedy dydaktyka akademicka jest nowoczesna: o potrzebie dywersyfikacji kształcenia na odległość", *Kultura i Polityka, 16*, 45–63.
(in press) "The shallows and the depths. Cognitive and social presence in blended tutoring".

Studies in Computer Assisted Language Learing

Edited by Anna Turula

Vol. 1 Anna Turula/Maria Chojnacka (eds.) : CALL for Bridges between School and Academia. 2015.

Vol. 2 Mariusz Marczak/Jarosław Krajka (eds.): CALL for Openness. 2016.

www.peterlang.com

www.ingramcontent.com/pod-product-compliance
Ingram Content Group UK Ltd.
Pitfield, Milton Keynes, MK11 3LW, UK
UKHW041829100926
8556IPUK00002B/89